979.03   NES   20905
NESTER
First half of my life

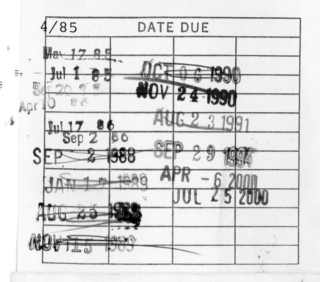

4

Homer Public Library

141 West Pioneer Avenue

Homer, Alaska   99603

FIRST HALF OF MY LIFE
by Paul M. Nester

WILLAMETTE PRESS
Post Office Box 2065
Beaverton, Oregon 97075

Library of Congress Cataloging in
Publication Data

Nester, Paul M. (Paul Michael), 1900-
First Half of my life.

Summary: The author recounts the first
forty-one years of his life, during
which he worked as a miner, served in
the navy, learned to fly, was a deputy
sheriff, and had experiences in Alaska
and Central America.

1. Nester, Paul M. (Paul Michael),1900-
2. United States--Biography. [1.Nester,
Paul M. (Paul Michael), 1900- 2. United
States--Biography.
I. Title.
CT275. N455A33 1983 979'.03'0924 [B] [92]
83-50325

ISBN 0-913695-00-9
ISBN 0-913695-01-7 (pbk.)

ABOUT THE AUTHOR

Read the book!

Paul Nester recuperated from a heart attack when he was 79 years old. After having a pace-maker installed, he is now able to swim, hunt and fish once again. For the benefit of his daughter, Margaret Ann Walters, his thirteen grand and great grandchildren, as well as for his other relatives and friends, he joined a writing class at the Beaverton Senior Citizen's Center and learned to write well enough to produce the <u>First Half of my Life.</u>

CONTENTS

ACKNOWLEDGEMENTS

Thanks to my wife, Katherine, for her loyal support and encouragement for well over 50 years. To my daughter, Margaret Ann, her husband, Fliegle, and my granddaughter Marianne (Annie) Walters for their continual encouragement for me to learn to write.

To Monica and Al Shaw, Pauline and Hugh Nester, Bob and Cleo Danaher for their continued support and for their part in the First Half of My Life.

To Diane Imel, former teacher of the Creative Writing Class at the Beaverton Senior Citizen's Center, whose expertise and patience made it possible for me to learn to write . . . and for her help editing. To each of the members of her class, whose critiquing was so very important.

To all my grandchildren, Kathi, Mary, Annie, Karin, Cecilia, John and Paul, for their help and encouragement. And especially to Mary for her art-work creating the logo for my stationery and the cover for this book. To Kathy for her help with the brochure and most important, to John, whose many weeks of work, helping in the editing and in the actual production of this book made it possible.

To my good friend, Hugh Sparks, for his all-around help and support . . . and to all the other friends whose help and encouragement I sincerely appreciate.

CHAPTER 1

EARLY DAYS IN PORTLAND

1900 - 1914

One day, when I was about two or three years old, I wandered off towards Mississippi Avenue. I was fascinated by the streetcar track and the occasional car that would pass. Down the street was a building with swinging doors where men kept going in and coming out. The doors swung back and forth every time anyone passed. One day, out of curiosity, I walked right under those doors.

It was a smoky, noisy place, full of men talking and drinking at a long counter. A man picked me up and set me at the end of the counter where there was all kinds of food. Another man asked if anyone knew me. . .no one answered. He then tried to get me to tell my name. . .but I couldn't talk. They started feeding me crackers, cheese and pickles. I was hungry, so I ate my fill.

In the meantime, Mother and my sister Phyrn, with the help of the neighbors, had been looking everywhere for me. Directly across the street from our house was a deep gulch. In the rainy season, there was a lake where several drownings had occurred. Since I was an inquisitive child, my mother was sure I would be found at that lake. She didn't think of looking anywhere else, let alone a saloon.

Before long another man came through the swinging doors. Ordering himself a drink, he looked at me. Then he asked the bartender, "Where's Tom Nester?" After a short explanation by the bartender, this man took me home. I learned that he worked with my father on the railroad and knew our family.

But wait! Let me go back and start at the beginning.

I was born in Portland, Oregon, August 17, 1900. My sister Phyrn was three years older than I. We were both born and raised in a two story house on Wheeler street, a few hundred yards north of where the Memorial Coliseum now stands. Along about 1904, my folks purchased an acre of land in Upper Albina, on Fremont street at the foot of Haight.

The property had an old house, a barn and a wood shed. The pride of that place was its fine old orchard. We had most every kind of fruit one could desire. The location of our new land was well out in the suburbs. There were no sidewalks. The streets were dirt roads in the summer and mud holes in the winter. Now Mother wouldn't have to worry about that gulch. . .or my going to a saloon. Not for awhile anyway.

It didn't take Dad long to get that place in shape. A garden plot was worked up and soon, we had all the vegetables, fruit and berries we needed.

That house wasn't very comfortable, so Mother and Dad had a new one built. It was a lovely two story family home, complete with basement and fireplace. There was electricity, too. Up until that time, side-wall gas fixtures furnished our lights. We were all happy in our

8

Forestry Building at the Lewis and Clark Fair
Portland, Oregon
1905

new home. Dad rented out the old house and the new tenants were good renters. This gave Dad an idea. From that time on, when he found something good, in a house or a lot, and if he had the money or could arrange it, he would buy. The houses would be cleaned up, painted, then rented. The lots, he would build on, then rent. This became a most profitable side-line.

In 1905, when I was five, Mother took us kids to the Lewis and Clark Fair. What impressed me most was the huge Forestry Building. It was constructed with unhewn logs cut from virgin forest. Starting from the base, with logs of four or five feet diameter, they ascended to the second and third heights, finishing with logs of from twelve to eighteen inches. That building was a giant! It was the only structure from the Fair to remain on its original site for many years after the Fair was over.

In this magnificent building, Phyrn was fascinated by a red-colored glass cup on exhibit. Mother bought it for her and, to this day, it's still in the family.

One sunday morning, our family had just returned from church. I still had my brand new suit on. The kids in the neighborhood were having a big time walking with their stilts through a large mud puddle in the middle of the street. I got my stilts and joined in the fun. Right in the middle of that puddle, one of my stilts went straight down! After wallowing in the mud, I finally made my way out. Now I ask you, how do you square a deal like that with your parents?

When I was old enough, Phyrn took me to school. Saint Mary's Catholic School was located behind the church on the corner of William's and Stanton. It was not quite one mile from home. At that time, as far as I was concerned, the only reason I went, was because my parents made me! I thought there were so many other,

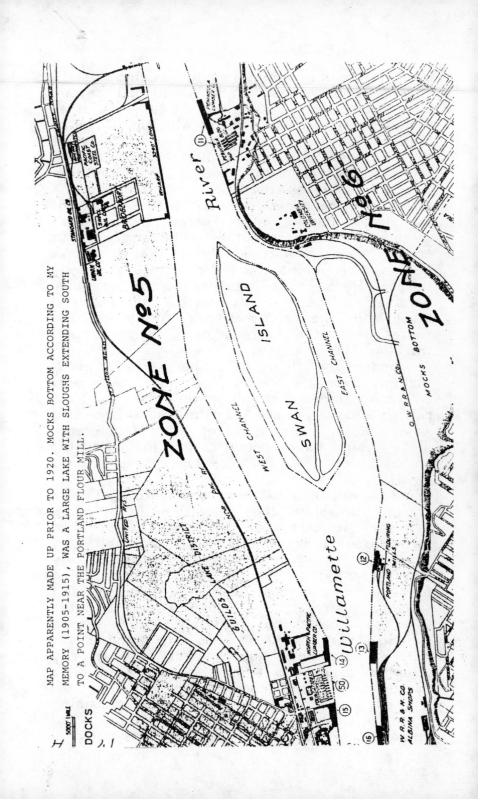

MAP APPARENTLY MADE UP PRIOR TO 1920. MOCKS BOTTOM ACCORDING TO MY
MEMORY (1905-1915), WAS A LARGE LAKE WITH SLOUGHS EXTENDING SOUTH
TO A POINT NEAR THE PORTLAND FLOUR MILL.

DOCKS

ZONE Nº5

ZONE Nº6

River

Willamette

SWAN ISLAND

WEST CHANNEL

EAST CHANNEL

MOCKS BOTTOM

COLUMBIA UNIVERSITY

LAKE DISTRICT

GUILDS LAKE

PORTLAND FLOURING MILLS

O.W.R.R.&N.CO.

W.R.R.&N.CO.
ALBINA SHOPS

PACIFIC COAST STEEL CO.

STANDARD OIL CO.

BROADWAY

500 FT 1 MILE

more interesting things I could be doing.

We had a cousin who vacationed at our home each summer. Guy was three years older than I so Mother trusted him with me. Guy was quite a "guy"! It wasn't long after his arrival that we made our first exploration trip to the Willamette River. Guy and I went through Overlook, entered the woods and followed the trail down the canyon. We passed the shacks of the hobo jungle and crossed the railroad tracks. To get across the slough at the south end of Mock's Bottom, there was a narrow walkway on pilings which led across to Sandy Bottom. Here was a beautiful beach--a regular paradise on the river just north of the Portland Flour Mill. The kids from Lower Albina took the route across the railroad yards then through the Flour Mill property.

Under the flour mill, there was a plank walkway over the water. You could reach most any point under that mill on these planks. Here catfish and carp were plentiful. All one needed was hook, line and a bit of bait. If you were lucky, you'd have enough catfish for a fish-fry on the beach. What could be better after a good swim?

On one trip to the river with Guy, we started crossing the slough on the plank walkway. We were about half way across, when we met four kids, all near Guy's age and size. They were going in the opposite direction. Guy and I crawled off onto the tops of some piling to allow them to pass. But . . . they weren't satisfied with this . . . they wanted a fight! Guy was knocked into the slough! All four were leaning over, watching him struggle in the water, laughing. Nobody was paying any attention to me, so I found a good stick on a nearby piling and knocked the kid that had toppled Guy into the water. The remaining three boys caught me, took me to the shore and dunked me repeatidly. I thought I was going to drown! I give them credit though. They probably thought I was too little to know how to swim . . . that's why they took me ashore. I'll never forget that day and I don't think Guy will either! By the time that summer was over, I could swim quite well.

We always could tell when Dad was about to arrive home. He was a conductor for the Oregon, Washington Railroad and Navigation Company. His run was from Portland to Pendleton, Oregon. As his train came down through Sullivan's Gulch from the east, the engineer would let go with an unusual whistle. That was their signal. When we heard that, we knew that within an hour or two Dad would be home. Sometimes it meant, "get your work done fast, or you'll be in for it," but most of the time, it just meant "Hurrah, Dad's back home!"

Late that summer, our family went on a boat trip up the Willamette. We were invited by friends at Jenning's Landing, people who had a sailboat. The boat was large enough to carry our two families. Sailing south, we passed several interesting islands and finally anchored in a beautiful cove. It was a place, just right for swimming before lunch. Like everyone else, I put my bathing suit on and dived over the side. Mother screamed! . . . Until then, she didn't know that I could swim! . . . She soon found out where and when I learned and that, of course, put Guy in a bad light. When we got home, she took me aside and told me that though she would never forbid my going to the river to swim or explore, I had to have a good reason and she wanted me to ask for her permission. This I promised to do. It worked out great for the both of us.

On April 18, 1906 a terrible earthquake hit San Francisco. One evening at supper, Mother and Dad were talking about it. Dad had an idea. "How'd you all like to take a trip down to the depot in the morning? The train from San

Francisco comes in just about the time I leave for Pendleton and it might be interesting to see those people who made their escape. In the morning, we all can go down to the depot."

When the train arrived from San Francisco, our whole family was at the Portland depot. There was a big crowd of people. As the incoming passengers entered the station, it was easy to spot those who came from San Francisco. Those poor people! They had made their escape in such a hurry that they had no time to be concerned about proper clothing. They wore what they could grab and quite a few were wrapped in railroad-donated blankets. The blankets not only gave warmth but made pretty good overcoats as well. As they met their friends and relatives, the strain on the survivors faces rapidly disappeared. Now, they could start again . . . in safety.

At his job, Dad had worked his way up to passenger train conductor. One cold winter day, when he arrived home from one of his trips, all of us kids, as usual, made a rush to meet him. After greetings, Dad said, "Paul, why don't you see what I have in my overcoat pocket." I put my hand in his pocket and felt something alive! There, was the cutest little puppie I ever did see. Dad explained that after everyone had departed and he made his inspection trip through the train, he found this little fellow cuddled in the corner of a seat. We kids named the puppy 'Shep' and he grew up to fit that name. For many years he was our loyal friend.

My brother Hugh was about two and a half years younger than I. On one occasion, he wandered off into the woods with a neighbor boy and Shep and got lost. After going around and around, Hugh decided It might work if he told Shep to go home. "Go home Shep, go home!" Shep took off with the boys running behind. He led them directly home.

About that time, Annie, my father's youngest sister, came to live with us. She was great with us kids and a mighty big help for mother. For us, she was, something like a second mother, only Annie wasn't so strict. She didn't have to be. After all, we weren't her responsibility.

During the winter months, Mother had been contracting pneumonia. Dad tried to solve the problem. About the time the bad weather started, Dad would take his vacation. He would get train passes for the entire family and take us to Southern California. From 1906 until 1910, we spent the winter months in Pamona, Long Beach, Los Angeles and in Santa Monica. My youngest sister, Monica, was born in Santa Monica, March 20, 1910.

The summer I turned eight, my parents decided I should learn something about life on a farm. Visiting my cousins, Henry and Ida Cromer at Springwater, I learned a bit about farm life. Most of my time, however, was spent fishing in nearby Clear Creek where trout and craw-fish were plentiful.

One thing I will never forget happened on the farm. My cousin Alberta was just three years old. She was pretty, the only child in the family and her father's pride and joy. Suddenly Alberta became ill. Her mother sent me to fetch her father, Henry, who was working in the field. I returned with him on the run! He took one look and immediately phoned the doctor in Estacada (six miles away). I overheard him say "Run those horses! If you kill them, I'll pay for them." Before long, the doctor pulled in the driveway with a team of frothing animals and ran to the house! Henry told me to take care of the horses. I walked the panting team until the doctor came out. He had treated Alberta for ptomaine poisoning. The doctor knew his business. Today, in Estacada,

Alberta York is alive and well.

My brother, Hugh, grew up to be somewhat of a problem for me. Everywhere I would go, he'd follow. At first, I did all I could to "ditch" him, but he was persistant. He would not give up. Eventually, he won and in time, I got used to his companionship. Together we explored the woods and fished and swam in the Willamette River.

My first bicycle was purchased for $7.50 from a school acquaintance . . . and that was hard earned money. When I got home, I gave Hugh a ride on the handlebars. We hit a bump and the frame of the bike folded up. Upon inspection, I found it had been broken before and was patched up to make it saleable. That sure taught me a lesson. However it wasn't a total loss . . . with a new frame, the bike lasted for many more years.

Early one spring, my folks agreed to a proposition. I'd buy a rooster and twelve hens and build a chicken house. They'd finance me. Caring for the flock was my responsibility and I could sell the eggs to the family for 25 cents a dozen. The deal worked out well. I was in business and now I could make my own spending money.

Claude Lampert, who lived nearby was one of my best friends. His father had built a shop above their garage. It was equipped with a blacksmith forge, machines and tools. Claude was a pretty fair mechanic for his age and he was teaching me. Some of the bows, arrows, knives and tomahawks we turned out were superior. Once, we built a cannon out of a piece of one inch pipe! The powder came from firecrackers. We tried it out in the basement of a nearby unoccupied house. To our surprise, the blast took out the middle support post in that basement! I don't know whether we hit our target or not, but that explosion created quite a stir in the neighborhood!

Uncle Jim was my Dad's brother. He was a sawyer in a lumber mill in Everett, Washington. Each year at Christmas time, he'd take his vacation and come to visit for a week or so. When he arrived, he was always loaded with gifts for the family. When I was nine, or maybe ten, Jim brought Hugh and I a set of boxing gloves. He was also well qualified to teach us a few tricks with them. My trouble was that Hugh was too small to be a fair match, so I tried each of the neighbor boys. They were more my size and age and I got quite a bit of good practice. One day Vince Keegan and his mother came to visit. Vince wanted to try the gloves with me. Unfortunately, he ended up with a bloody nose! I had no idea it would cause such a "hubbub". It came close to ruining my Mother's friendship with Mrs. Keegan.

On one of our trips back from Sandy Bottom, Hugh and I found some railroad signal torpedoes. They're about the size of a silver dollar with spring clips attached so that they can be secured to a rail. The torpedo contains an explosive cap (made for noise effect only). When an engine runs over it, the blast signals the engineer and transmits a message to him. We took the torpedoes home and it didn't take us boys long to find a use for them . . . the Russell Streetcar line ran right near our house along Commercial Avenue.

One day, we secreted all the kids in the neighborhood in a good position for observation. A torpedo was placed on the streetcar tracks nearby. When the car passed over the torpedo, the explosion was all we had hoped for . . . and more! That car stopped almighty fast and the passengers frantically spilled out! They all must have thought that the motor of that car had exploded! Some minutes later, after the motorman had inspected the motor, they returned to the car and it proceeded on its way undamaged. Now, if we used good judgement we kids could have one heck of a time . . . after all, we had several torpedoes left!

As time passed, Upper Albina was becoming more like a "grown-up" city. By 1909 or 1910, Williams Avenue at Russell Street was like downtown Portland. From Morris street north, it had been corduroy plank and mud. Now there was gravel, at least in the middle of the road. Sidewalks were replacing bicycle paths most everywhere . . . even on Fremont street. The blacksmith shop next to the livery stable on Vancouver Avenue, just north of Russell street, was starting to repair cars. I don't think I liked all those changes . . . they were coming too fast.

One summer Dad asked me if I would like to go to Pendleton with him. The idea had occurred to me before but I had dismissed it as being impossible. For several years, ever since Dad had become a passenger train conductor, his trips were much more regular. Now that we could depend on his schedule, I was glad to go with him!

When we got to the depot, the train was on the loading tracks. Dad had work to do, so he left me in one of the cars where the 'Peanut Butcher' made his headquarters. A Peanut Butcher is a salesman who peddles candy, popcorn, etc. The passengers started loading and soon we were underway. It wasn't long before Dad came by the car to see that I was getting along all right. By this time I had become acquainted with the brakeman and the Peanut Butcher. They treated me in a friendly manner and I was enjoying every minute of it.

The train had crossed the Willamette River and was heading up Sullivan's Gulch. Before long, it made it's way through the Columbia Gorge. I found a good seat on the river-side and spent most my time at the window . . . the

18

scenery was breathtaking! Sometimes the train would slow down and packages or bundles of papers, mail and supplies would be tumbled off. If you watched long enough, someone would appear sooner or later to rescue his belonging's. Several short stops were made at stations along the way. At Hood River, The Dalles and some of the other towns, the stop was long enough for me to get off the train and stretch my legs.

The eastern section terminal of the train line was at Pendleton. After we arrived and Dad completed his work, we checked into the railroaders hotel, cleaned up and had a fine supper. Later that evening, Dad took me to the local nichelodean.

Early the next morning we were on the train heading back to Portland. The dining car meals were still great and except for a few details, it was the day before in reverse. As the train made it's way down the Columbia River Gorge, Dad came through the car and motioned for me to follow him. The train was slowing down. The step coverings in one of the cars had been raised and Dad made his way down to the lower step. In a remote area, the train passed a man who was holding what appeared to be a tennis racket. Dad leaned out and as the train passed, put his arm through the racket . . . it had no webbing. A heavy sack was attached. It was pulled in and the bag dropped to the floor of the car. The steps were closed and the sack opened. Dad said "Take a look." I peeked in and saw two beautiful salmon. "The man you saw holding the racket is a fisherman who operates a fish-wheel on the river. We shop for him, bring him his mail, supplies and newspapers and he keeps us supplied with salmon . . . one for the engineer and one for me." Now, I know where the "good fishing hole" that Dad talked about when he brought home the salmon is located.

19

One summer day, our neighbors, the Foresters, invited Phyrn and I to go on a camping trip. Mr. Forester was an engineer for the OWR & N. He had a vacation coming and he loved to fish. His wife and daughter, Doris, (about Phyrn's age), would be going. Phyrn couldn't go but I was glad to accept. Mr. Forester had asked a friendly engineer to stop his train not far east of Cascade Locks at Tanner Creek. It only took a few seconds for our party to scramble off with our camping equipment.

We packed our gear about one half mile up the creek and made camp. In those days, Tanner Creek was hard to reach except by railroaders. It was a great place to go on a vacation and ideal for fishermen! Even before the camp was thoroughly set up, Doris and I caught all the trout we needed for supper.

One day, Doris and I went on an exploration trip. We hiked back to the railroad and followed the tracks. As we approached the mouth of a tunnel, a train emerged and bore down on us! I jumped off the tracks and when I sensed Doris had not followed, I glanced back . . . there she was, <u>frozen</u> in the middle of the tracks! The train's whistle blew repeatedly but she just stood there . . . <u>rigid</u>! I made a flying leap and knocked her off the tracks! When the train passed, Doris managed to collect herself and after a short rest, we returned to camp. Doris told her parents what had happened. They were surprised but, at that time, didn't make much to-do about it. Later, however, after the fishing trip, I heard plenty. It seems both Doris and I were recognized by the train's engineer and fireman.

One day when I was working with Dad in the garden, he asked me, "If I bought a cow, would you take care of it and do the milking?" We would have all the milk and butter we could use and if there's any extra you could sell it to the neighbors. Besides, you wouldn't have so much grass to cut." It looked like a good deal to me, so I agreed. With lumber left from the barn, we built a cow shed and Dad purchased 'Daisy', a very fine Jersey. From that day on, my chores kept me pretty busy. I had no trouble selling the extra milk and the money I earned came in handy. Right away, I started Hugh in on the milking so that, in a pinch, he could take over for me.

In March or April, when the smelt ran in the Sandy River, Mom and Dad would take us kids up to Troutdale for a picnic. Most every time we would get our limit. The cleaning of those little fish, however, would become monotonous and boring. Most of the smelt we smoked in our back yard. They were delicious that way, and if we were lucky, we'd have enough to last through the year.

Crown Point, the Oregon lookout point below the Columbia Gorge, was constructed in 1913. That year, Claude Lampert, Cal Hoffmiller and I took a trip there on our bicycles. The road was rough and, just before we arrived, Claude hit a bump and broke the frame of his bike. Way out there, there was no way it could be fixed. He walked the mile or so to Crown Point and, after spending an hour or two seeing what we could see, we headed back home . . . three boys on two bikes, lugging along the third. It was tough going for a good long ways, but we made it.

Cal and I lived on the same block, his house was on the corner of Commercial and Ivy so we attended the same grade school and we were in the same class. His hobbies were mechanical in nature and his interest was in electricity. By the time he was twelve or thirteen years old, Cal was building wireless and crystal radio sets that could pick up signals from afar . . . an accomplishment practically unheard of in those days. I spent

21

many quiet hours in his shop with the earphones on, trying to tune in on something from far away.

When I was twelve years old, I started spending my vacations in Eastern Oregon. My grandfather, John Howell, had a homestead there, about five miles from Wamic. Dad would take me on his train up the Columbia as far as Bigg's Junction. There, I would transfer to the branch line that ran south on the east side of the Deschutes River. I would get off at Sherrer's Ferry and take the stage from there to Wamic. The stage I took was sort of a modernized version of the old timer coaches. It was an interesting two or three hour ride up through Tygh Valley. On this trip, I experienced my first real thrill with Indians. They rode their cayuses alongside the stage as it journeyed towards Wamic. They were just riding along for the company.

Grandpa drove his wagon in to pick me up and also to shop at Wamic. I think he was always just as happy to see me as I was to see him. His place was like the typical Oregon homestead--a small house and fairly large barn. The fences on his property were the old zig-zag type of split rail used by the earliest pioneers. He had 160 acres, about half in grain crops and the rest in small timber. The house was located at the edge of a stand of small pine trees. The trees became very thick and quite large as you went west into the forest. To the east were fields of grain. One forty acre plot of wheat was just ready for harvesting. Grandpa hitched the team to a binder (a harvesting machine which cut and tied bundles of wheat) and drove, while the machine cut and bound the wheat into small bundles. I helped shock those bundles, that is, make stacks or piles of ten or twelve bundles each in an upright position so the heads of wheat could cure.

At Grandpa's place I had my first encounter

with a rattlesnake. Out behind the barn, some scattered boards needed piling. I picked up one of the boards and a snake was underneath! He started to rattle! I ran a short distance, picked up a shovel, returned and cut that rattler in two! I saved the rattles and skin to take home as souvenirs . . . and those weren't the only souvenirs I took home. Grandpa had a little dog called "Sparky." He and I would go on trips of exploration. He was great company. On one trip, he was ahead of me and spotted something in a small clearing. He started barking and circling. Picking a good place from which to watch, I saw a large rattler coiled and ready to strike. Sparky kept circling . . . then he stopped barking and moved in closer. All of a sudden, after what seemed like the longest time, Sparky made a false move (like he was going after the snake). The snake struck . . . just what Sparky had been waiting for. He side-stepped the strike and caught the rattler in mid-air, directly behind its head and proceeded to bite and shake it to death!

One day, Grandpa took me on a trip. The famous old Barlow Road ran through his place so we followed it west, perhaps a mile and a half, to a place he called the Toll Gate. Descending the grade to the valley floor, the road made a 90° turn to the right. It crossed in front of a house and large barn, then went on for two hundred yards or so across the valley floor, finally crossing Gate Creek. On the other side of the creek, it made another 90° turn and continued its route west over the Cascades. A giant cottonwood tree stood shading the house near the first 90° turn in the road. Behind the house and near the canyon bank was the barn. The lush growth on that valley floor was exemplary of the rich soil. It would have made a beautiful painting or photo.

Grandpa said, "Paul, this is the 'Old

Strickland Place.' It was the home of your Great Grandparents, William and Elizabeth Strickland. They lived here for many years . . . they died here too. I thought you should know."

Grandpa spent several hours visiting the people who now resided there. While he visited, I explored the area . . . my imagination running wild.

As we approached the house on our return to Grandpa's place, a saddle horse was hitched to the rack. "Looks like we have company." When we entered the house, I was introduced to one of the neighbors, Sam Cooper, who lived about ten miles away. Sam was sitting in a chair in the kitchen and didn't look good.

"John, I've had this dam toothache for three days and it won't go away."

Grandpa took a look at Sam's tooth and said, "Yes . . . it should come out." Taking a bottle of whiskey from the cupboard, he handed it to Sam. While they visited, Sam did as much drinking as talking. When Grandpa figured Sam had about enough, he left to get his forceps. When he returned, he told Sam to hold on. Sticking them into Sam's mouth, he yanked out a mighty nasty looking snag. Holding it up, he said, "Take a look!" Sam was drunk, minus one bad tooth . . . but happy!

Too soon, my vacation had come to an end. On my trip home, I took the train from Sherrer's Falls. We traveled down the east bank of the Deschutes River. When the conductor came by, he took a seat beside me and pointed out the right of way across the river on the west side and explained, "For some years not too long ago, when this railroad was being built, we had competition. There was a race for the right to operate a railroad into Bend. Two companies were anxious to get all the trade from the interior of Oregon. The Hill Railroad Dynasty, which controlled railroads in the State of Washington, was competing with the Harriman People, who operated the Union Pacific in Oregon. It's hard to believe that REAL battles were fought along this river. There was shooting . . . and several workmen on each side of the river lost their lives. It's so peaceful and beautiful now, that it's hard to believe there was bloodshed here!

John Strand, was a friend of mine who lived nearby. The winter of 1912-13, the two of us decided to build a canoe. Since neither of us had ever done this before, we went to the library on Knott street and read books that told us how. We worked (in our spare time) all through that winter. We scouted for wooden barrel hoops, long thin strips from lumber mills, paint, putty and canvas. Good canvas was hard to come by, so we finally had to settle for older and poorer canvas. When you consider that canoe cost us nothing, that's not too bad. When it was completed, we christened it the "War-horse."

The first nice days of spring arrived and with the help of Hugh and John's young brother Chris, we hauled our "War-horse" down to Sandy Bottom. John, Hugh and I got in and headed for Swan Island. Our "seaworthy" canoe started to leak and Hugh started to bail while John and I paddled faster and faster! By the time we reached mid-channel, our War-horse was AWASH! We all went overboard, swimming and pushing our canoe all the way to Swan Island. We emptied the canoe of water and pulled it ashore near the southern tip of the island. Scouting around, we found tar on the beach. Some other kids had a fire going, so we borrowed some coals to start our own fire and melted the tar in a can we had found. When the tar was melted, we gave the bottom of the canoe a thick coat. Not satisfied, we made another trip for more tar. When finished, the bottom of our canoe had its second coat and it never leaked again.

In those days, Swan Island was a real island over a mile long and about a half mile wide. It was a primitive place covered with brush and woods . . . a great place for boys to explore. Along its shores were wonderful places to camp and to fish. With the "War-horse" in the summer, what more would a 12 year old boy dream about?

One big problem we faced was, where to keep our prize. There was no way we could pack it back and forth from home. So we decided to hide it in the brush, along the edge of the slough at Mock's Bottom. Sometimes, we would sink it, but rocks heavy enough to hold it down were hard to come by.

Then, one day along towards autumn, we lost our prize! Someone had found the hiding place and stole our canoe! We never did see the "War-horse" again. But, the following winter, not to be defeated, John and I built "War-horse #2." It was a much better boat and we were able to find a safer "hiding" place.

All the larger river and ocean boats used the channel east of Swan Island. For us, this was great. When we saw a river boat coming, we would hurriedly paddle out, hoping that it would be a stern wheeler. They would leave a wake of rollers for several miles. When the boat passed, we paddled into the waves and enjoyed a roller coaster ride that would last for ten or fifteen minutes. It was great fun.

My Mother's sister, Florence, lived in Vancouver, Washington. That was one of our favorite places to visit. Hugh and I would get permission, take our bikes, and head north on Vancouver Avenue. On our way to the ferry boat landing on the Columbia, we passed woods and sloughs. The ferry boat charge was 25¢ but the ride was always worth it. Aunt Florence always welcomed us . . . she understood boys and would have lots of good things on hand for us to eat. After visiting a few hours, we would be on our way back home. If there was time, we would fish in one of the sloughs along the way.

Williams Avenue at Russell Street was the center of Upper Albina's business area. The first nichelodian I remember was on the north side of Russell just west of Williams. They had music and vaudville on saturday nights and it only cost five cents. Some years later, the Tivoli theater was built on Williams Avenue, just south of Russell. It was more modern and the cost was ten cents. There were many stores and offices nearby. Canard and Adams was perhaps the largest department store. There was no need to go all the way to Portland to shop since you could get most anything there.

A fire station was located east of Williams on Russell. If you were lucky enough to be close by when a fire call came in, you could see the fast harnessing of the trained horses, the lighting of the fire in the steam engine and the rapid take-off . . . all bells ringing! After seeing that once, you would never forget it!

During the winter in Albina, when the snow and ice would cooperate, bob-sledding on Russell street hill was the thing. Everybody turned out. Most of the sleds would travel all the way to Mississippi Avenue in Lower Albina. There would always be someone posted on the tracks to flag down any streetcar (in case one came along). The motormen were most cooperative.

In June, 1914, I graduated from Saint Mary's grade school. Cal Hoffmiller, Frank Stopper and Steve Eberle also graduated. That summer I worked pretty hard, cleaning up and painting places Dad was getting ready to rent. When it was time to start school in the fall, needless to say, I was very happy!

National Guard Armory. Portland, Oregon.

CHAPTER 2

HIGH SCHOOL YEARS

1914 – 1917

Jefferson High School, about one mile from home, was my choice. Phyrn went there too, so we always walked to school together. We became better friends because of that . . . we traded confidences.

Physically, I was in pretty good shape and fairly large for my age, so I decided to go out for wrestling. I liked it and did quite well at it . . . that is, until an unusual thing happened. The wrestling mats became infected and all the wrestlers got the 'Seven Year Itch.' I'll bet it was seven months before I got rid of that itch, and for years after, anyone who dared to scratch around the Jefferson territory would be accused of being a wrestler.

Along about this time, the Oregon National Guard decided to recruit a company from the students attending Jefferson. Recruiters talked at school assemblies and paid visits to the gym and to many of the other classes. Their efforts were successful. Enough students were interested to organize a company. Though John Strand and I were both big enough, we were nowhere near the 16 year old age limit. We managed to obtain age waivers to take home for our parent's signatures. You should have heard my Mom and Dad . . . no way would they sign . . . no way would they give their consent! John's parents, however, did sign.

When I told the officer in charge what happened, he said, "That's tough, but you just come along . . . sort of fill in without signing up. We're short on manpower and you can help us in that way."

Both John and I were issued uniforms and all the equipment a national guardsman needed. From then on, I attended every drill and went on weekend training trips. I even qualified with a Springfield rifle as a sharpshooter at Camp Withcombe, the Clackamas Rifle Range. Along with the others, I went through the whole bit . . . and I liked it.

During the winter of 1914-15, I took over a Journal paper route in Woodlawn. My territory was everything east of Union Avenue and north of Dekum Street. It was considered a large route and took all my spare time (after school, of course). I was lucky to be home by six o'clock, so Hugh took over the milking and my other duties at home. I worked hard getting my route into shape. By summer, my route had more customers than it ever had and I had two boys helping me with the deliveries.

That June, Phyrn graduated from Jefferson High. The celebration was hardly over when she married John Danaher, a neighbor boyfriend. Phyrn and John were happy, but our folks were disappointed. They thought the "kids" should have waited for awhile.

Towards the end of summer 1915, I was able to take another vacation in Eastern Oregon. Besides visiting my grandparents, I had another idea. The year before, I had become friends with Mamie and Jim Keniwick, old friends of my Mother. They operated a pretty good size cattle outfit in the Wamic Area. I wanted to work on that ranch during my vacation and Jim gave me the opportunity.

Early one morning, Jim and I headed for the mountains with our saddle horses and six pack animals loaded with supplies for the summer herder and salt for the cattle. Most of the way, we followed the Old Barlow Road up the White River Valley. It was beautiful country to travel and I enjoyed every minute of it.

In the late afternoon, we arrived at our destination. After unloading the camp supplies at the herder's cabin, we went to a high ridge which over-looked the White River. This was the cattle salting place. We unpacked the blocks of salt and distributed them over an acre or more at intervals. When finished, Jim went out on the tip of the ridge, where he could see for miles in every direction. He started calling . . . "Ya Hoo . . . Ya Hoo!" In the distance, clouds of dust would form. Soon, you could make out small groups of white-faced Herford cattle, making their way towards us. There were thousands of cattle rapidly heading for the salt blocks! Jim, mounted and with a smile, said, "Guess we better take these pack animals back over to the corral (located near the herder's cabin)." I felt better when I got off our spot on the ridge. That scene, was the closest thing to a Buffalo Stampede that I had ever seen.

That evening, after a good supper, Jim and the herder talked. They exchanged news and then (for my benefit) started telling stories. Their stories were interrupted by a sudden lightning storm, with thunder for emphasis. I was so tired that night that I slept soundly . . . in spite of it all.

Next morning, we were up early. After breakfast, we went out on the point where the cattle were licking the salt blocks. They had been busy all through the night . . . the salt

31

was half gone.

Another reason for our trip to the point lookout: We were able to spot three columns of smoke . . . fires started from last night's electrical storm! I could see that both men were concerned. We rode back towards the cabin and, as we approached, another group of horsemen appeared. It was the local forest ranger with three men. They had several pack animals loaded with tools and supplies. The ranger wanted to draft all three of us to help fight the fires. After some discussion, he settled for one . . . me! After all, in case the fires got out of hand, a lot of cattle had to be headed out of that part of the country.

In short order, I was on my way with the forester and his crew, headed for the nearest fire. In two hours, we were there. The fire, less than an acre in size, was burning on the ridge top.

We immediately started cutting trees and brush and making sure that all we had cut fell towards the fire, inside a circle outlined by the forester. Then we started digging a ditch surrounding the fire. By dark, a fair ditch containing the fire had been dug. We ate our supper and turned in . . . all, that is, but the ranger. He must have worked through the night with the fire.

Next morning, after a speedy breakfast, we tackled it again. By noon, our surrounding ditch and clearing satisfied the ranger. After a good meal, the ranger said to me, "I'm going to leave you here to guard this fire. Keep it from jumping the line. You can brush out and widen the ditch area. We have a couple more fires to take care of. It might be four or five days, but don't worry, I'll be back for you!" They left me food supplies and took off.

All of a sudden I was alone. I had my horse and blanket, the food they had left and my .22 rifle which Jim had allowed me to bring.

The rest of that day, I worked harder than ever. I just didn't want that fire to get away from me, and it kept me from feeling alone. As it started to get dark, I cooked myself a nice meal. After eating my fill, I checked my horse and the fire and then "turned in." Until then, I had never been out like that . . . ALL ALONE. When I went to sleep, my .22 rifle was right by my side. I was so tired I slept soundly right through the night.

The next morning, I was up early and made a round of the fire. Thank goodness the weather had been favorable. The fire was as it should be, gradually burning out. I spent most of the day covering hot spots. There were plenty of them to cover so I put in a good day.

That night, after bedding down, I heard my first panther cry! It sounded like the cry of a woman in distress! It was scary! I kept thinking, "I wish I had my National Guard Springfield instead of this .22 rifle." I got up, moved my sleeping place closer to the fire and stirred it up so the flames would last longer. I also brought my horse in and tethered it nearby . . . after that, I slept well.

It was the fifth day before the ranger returned. The fire was practically out and so were my food supplies. After a thorough examination of the area, the ranger congratulated me on the job I had done. We packed up and in a couple of hours were back at the cattle herder's cabin. The ranger took my full name and address and told me that the U.S. Forest Service would send me a check for my work. He shook my hand, thanked me again, and was on his way.

I waited at the cabin the rest of the afternoon. When the herder returned, he was glad to see me. He told me Jim had pulled out with the pack animals two days before. He asked me if I thought I would have any trouble finding my way down the mountain to the

Keniwick's ranch alone. I assured him I would have no trouble. That evening, I enjoyed his cooking, his stories and a wonderful night's sleep.

Next morning, after a hearty breakfast, I mounted and was on my way down the mountain. The return trip was uneventful. After a short visit with the Keniwicks, I went on to Grandpa's where I spent another day or two just visiting and relaxing. By now, my time was up, so I headed for my Portland home where I had so much to tell.

After getting properly adjusted at home, the first thing I did was to check on my paper route. I was relieved . . . everything was in order. I had made a fine choice of boys to run things while I was gone. Now all I had to do was work hard to get more customers, so I could keep the two on permanently.

Then one day, early in March of 1916, I was in class at school when a student came around to the classes with a message: "EMERGENCY! All members of the National Guard, are to be excused from school immediately. Go to your homes, get into your uniforms and report to the Armory!"

It took a bit of doing to get into my home and get my uniform and when John and I arrived at the Armory, about one thousand other guardsmen were there. After awhile, our Company's top sergeant had us 'fall-in.' Our Captain addressed us: "Pancho Villa has raided American Territory. At Columbus, New Mexico, many Americans have been killed! We're going after him." The Captain called out six names and my name was one! "Thank you for helping us," he said, "but turn in your equipment and GO ON HOME."

I was a very disappointed boy . . . and that's putting it mildly. John's name had not been called, so he got to go. For months, I envied John and all the other National Guard friends. When he returned, he told me all about it. They had gone no further south than the border near Colexico. They had done nothing but 'guard duty' in that blazing desert . . . what a drag! Guess I was just lucky . . . thanks to my Mother and Dad.

One Friday, early in the spring of 1916, Dad was in a good humor. He asked me what I was going to be doing Saturday morning. I could think of nothing particular other than going out to my route and doing some work there. He asked me if I'd like to go out for a ride in a car. He went on to say a Maxwell salesman was bringing a car over and, if I was interested, I could go along for the ride. I was surprised and most certainly interested. I had no idea Dad was considering buying a car.

The Maxwell salesman arrived right on time with a sparkling new touring car. It was then I found out Dad had already purchased that car and was about to learn how to drive. In those days, when a salesman sold a car, it was his duty to teach the purchaser how to drive.

The salesman told Dad to get in the drivers seat. He got in alongside and I was told to get in the back. After some time explaining the mechanics and the instruments of operation, we got underway . . . jerk . . . jerk . . . jolt . . . bang . . . the car made two leaps and a jump, then stopped. I wondered whether or not I had made the right decision to take that ride. Again, the salesman went through the driving instructions. Dad tried once more and, this time, it turned out much better. However, there were times when I was concerned about Dad's ability to stop. It all worked out okay, though and after an hour or so, we were safely back home and the salesman made his departure.

Then Dad asked me if I would like to try it. Right from the start, I did fairly well. As time went by, I became the chief driver for the

35

family. From that time on, that car brought great pleasure to our family and to many of our friends. Hardly a week would go by, especially in periods when we had good weather, that we didn't go on a picnic or just go out for a ride. We went everywhere there were roads to go . . . and we loved it!

One morning (when I just happened to be at home) Dad received a telephone call. He had to catch a train in a hurry. Something had happened to the conductor who was supposed to take the train out. Dad called to me to get the car . . . FAST! As I drove out of the garage, he jumped in, his work clothes under his arm. He told me to drive fast as I could down to lower Albina, near the east end of the Steel Bridge. I did as he said, while he changed into his conductors uniform. A passenger train was crossing the bridge and the engine was already ahead of us as we paralleled the tracks. While it was still going, Dad jumped from the car and ran along-side the train. As the very last car passed, he swung aboard. Standing on the steps he turned and waved. Right there, in my mind, Dad's stock went up 100%..... I was very proud!

My father wasn't the only one I had great love and respect for. Mother shared equally. A wonderful mother to all of us children. She was a great cook and ran a home like most people dream about. Born in the Springwater area, just south of Estacada, Oregon, in 1877, she was a third generation Oregon pioneer. In those days, one had to fight hard to stay alive. She lost her mother when she was just seven years old and by the time she was twelve, she was working as a governess for the family of the Indian Agent at the Warm Springs Indian Reservation. There were three small children in that family and my mother wasn't so much older. You might say, they were all raised with the Indians . . . perhaps that's why mother understood the adventurous spirit of her first born son.

Fall classes were just starting and it was time to go back to school again. When I first started High School, my parents encouraged me to take a commercial business course and now that I was half way through. I could do a bit of typewriting, bookkeeping and printing. Of course, I took all the other necessary subjects, but I couldn't see the value of them. I thought, "No way would I spend my life doing any one of those three things." Guess I was disturbed . . . I just didn't know what I wanted.

For the past five or six years, I had been going to the library a lot . . . reading books on adventure and exploration. What could I take in school that would help me become what I wanted to be? Trouble is, I didn't quite know myself what that was. At times, I thought I might like to make a try for either West Point or Annapolis, but I was no prize student so that was almost impossible.

Another thing disturbing me was Cal Hoffmiller. He had gone to Benson Trade School and was well on his way to becoming an electrican. Then there was Harold Gorman . . . he was half way through his way to become a pattern-maker. With the commercial business course, what did I have? I was wasting my time. Why didn't I go to a trade school?

John and (my sister) Phyrn's first child, Johnnie was born January 14, 1917. I was asked to be Johnnie's Godfather. John's very attractive 15 year old sister, Katherine, was the Godmother. Little did I know that, some years later, Katherine would become my wife and best pal for well over fifty years!

Cordova, Alaska.

Jake Howell with his dog-team.

CHAPTER 3

ALASKA

1917 - 1918

I had a cousin, Genevive Strickland, who was married to a young civil engineer, Craig Redmond. Craig was a graduate from Columbia University (now the University of Portland). In 1916 and 1917, times were tough. Jobs were not easy to come by and this caused ups and downs for the newlyweds. Craig and I became quite good friends. He was six foot three, weighed 200 pounds and was five years older than I. We shared a love of hunting and fishing and he was good at both.

Genevive and I had an uncle, Jake Howell, an Alaskan mining man. Each year, he had been coming Outside (Continental United States) for vacation, arriving about Christmas and spending a month or more. We all enjoyed Jake and his Alaskan stories. Genevive had an idea . . . she asked Jake if there was a chance of a job up north. His answer was, "Sure, I could help Craig get started. It's too early now . . . nothing worthwhile will be opening up until after the Break-up (when the ice melts in the spring). It would be best for Craig to wait until March. That'll give him plenty of time to get in before the start of the season. You stay here until he gets established."

When I heard about Genevive and Craig's trip to Alaska, I had a hard time trying to put it out of my mind. I finally decided to do something. At my next opportunity, I asked Jake if he would help me get a job up north, too. I had the money for my fare and expenses (my paper route had been a good producer and I had saved) and I could go along with Craig. Jake's answer was "Yes, Paul, if you can get your parent's permission and if Craig will take you along." (I still think that he never believed my parents would let me go).

I was really excited but I knew I had to proceed with great care in obtaining my parents consent. To say they were shocked would be putting it mildly. They gave me every reasonable argument they could find . . . however, when they saw that I was really determined, they gave in. They had always been very fair in their dealings with me and they had confidence in me. Craig was also glad to hear that I could go . . . he wouldn't be quite so lonesome on that long trip north.

January and February went by in a flash. I had to find somebody to take over my paper route to make sure it was left in good hands. The Journal people had treated me well and they at least deserved that consideration.

My next hurdle was the business of quitting school. That went okay with the exception of Mrs. Curran, my home class teacher. Like my mother, she tried very hard to talk me out of going. I thanked her for her interest, but I was stubborn.

Our departure from Portland, March 7, 1917, was not as easy as I thought it would be. Mother, Phyrn and Genevive all came down to the depot to see us off. Soon, the train was underway. Craig and I settled down to try and enjoy our ride to Seattle. I remember how disappointed I was. It looked like three quarters of all the trees between Portland and Seattle had been cut down. Nothing but that stump land remained on both sides of the tracks for most of the way.

In Seattle, after registering at a hotel, we went to the Northern Outfitting Store that Jake had recommended. They specialized in outfitting Alaskans. Following the salesman's suggestions, the necessary clothing to carry us through the remainder of that winter and the coming summer was purchased. There were other things, too, of equal importance . . . nets and covers for protection against the mosquitos, etc.

The following day, we were aboard one of the U.S. Puget Sound ferries enroute to Vancouver, British Columbia. Passing between those beautiful San Juan Islands was a trip I shall never forget.

After our arrival in Vancouver, we found there was just enough time to make our transfer to the Canadian Steamship docks and board the ship for Alaska. That ship was larger and more streamlined than the ferry we had just taken. It looked a lot more like an ocean going vessel.

After we were shown to our stateroom and had stowed our baggage away, Craig and I made a ship's tour. As it would be our home for some days, we wanted to find out all we could. This passed some time. Before we were through, whistles were blowing and the engines were starting . . . the ship was about to get underway. We went up on the deck and sure enough, we were slowly pulling away from the dock.

Always, when a ship makes it's arrival or departure, there is great excitment. It was thrilling! There were so many things to see. All were important and, if you were lucky, you could remember a few.

The first day of our trip, we traveled

41

Paul Nester in cap, standing by a freighter.

The five freighters and their outfits;
we followed from Chitna to Fairbanks.

northwest through the Inside Passage. Vancouver Island was on our west side and the British Columbia Mainland with its hundreds of Islands to the east. The ship was modern in every way and was a pleasure . . . the water was calm and the scenery beautiful.

Just before noon the second day, we cleared the north end of Vancouver Island and started to cross Queen Charlotte Sound. The waters became choppy. When the dinner bell rang, Craig and I went to our state room, cleaned up and made our way to the dining room. As we entered, a man rushed by us. Craig and I shrugged, sat down at our table and ordered. While we were waiting to be served, we observed several others suddenly get up and leave the dining room in a real hurry. When the waiter set our orders on the table, I too, jumped up and exited in record time! I had my first experience of sea-sickness!

Our first port of call was Prince Rupert. It is located just north of the mouth of the Sheena River. The stop was a very short one. Here we debarked a few passengers and unloaded some freight.

After leaving Prince Rupert, we were soon in American waters once more. Traveling through the inland Straights and Canals, we paralleled the Alaskan Panhandle. This area is approzimately 100 miles wide and 400 miles long. Thousands of Islands make up over one half of this Alaskan territory. I don't know where in this world you would go to find more spectacular scenery! Traveling those fjords and forests, straights and sounds, passing so many sparkling islands was an experience never to be forgotten!

A few hours later, we arrived at Ketchikan. It is located on an island separated from the mainland by the Behm Canal and one of the largest salmon fishing ports. It has been known as the salmon capital of the world. It's also a great center for the timber industry. Tourists come from near and far to see the Indian Village with its totem poles . . . sportsmen come to take advantage of the marvelous hunting and fishing.

Several hours travel further north was Wrangell, much like Ketchikan. It had also been the site of an old Russian Fort, a Hudson Bay Trading Post and U.S. Army's Fort Wrangell. As at Ketchikan, we didn't go ashore here either.

At Juneau, the Capital of Alaska, we finally got a break. The ship would be staying several hours, so everybody went ashore. Juneau is situated on the mainland at the base of mighty snow covered mountains. All the important governmental agencies are located there. Nearby is the Alaskan-Juneau Gold Mines, a very large and successful operation since 1880. A short distance northwest, the Mendenhall Glacier is located and that "chunk of ice" is something to see! It's over fifty miles long!

From Juneau, we headed west. After about 100 miles, we were out in the open sea . . . the Gulf of Alaska. Fortunately, the weather was good, so the ocean travel was reasonably calm. However, it couldn't be compared with the Inside Passage. Two days later, we arrived at Cordova. The snow had either just recently fallen, or had not yet melted . . . it was everywhere. We actually felt like we really were in Alaska.

For many years, Cordova had been the shipping terminus for the copper which was mined at Kennicott, over 100 miles to the north.

Early the next morning, Craig and I departed on one of the Copper Railroad trains that transported ore from the mine. The passengers rode in the caboose. Except for one freight and baggage car, all the others were ore cars. Our destination was Chitna . . . just over half way to Kennicott.

Chitna was the southern terminus of the trail from Fairbanks. It was a small village with a trading post and facilities for freighting operations. Twice a week, a convoy of double-enders (sleds about ten feet long and three feet wide hauled by one horse and primarily used to transport freight) would arrive. They would stay overnight, pick up their loads and then be ready to depart for the interior. Good strong horses or mules were needed to haul the loads over the mountains. Five double-enders, loaded with 1600 pounds each, were leaving that day. Two freighters (men who handle the horses and deliver the freight) handled them. Craig and I decided to ship our baggage. Mine weighed forty pounds and it cost me forty dollars to ship. We could have ridden on the double-enders, but the price ($1.00 per pound) was too steep for us. Instead, we walked in the trail broken by the double-enders.

At Cordova, we had been advised about the use of our Alaskan clothing. We were all rigged out in our winter gear.

The trail had been used all through that winter and was well broken in. Only a few inches of snow had fallen recently so there was no serious problem breaking trail. We gradually climbed as we headed towards the mountains . . . up rugged canyons and, occasionally through heavy timber. It was interesting country and all very beautiful. At noon, we stopped for lunch which had been prepared for us at Chitna. One of the freighters broke out a kerosine stove, gathered some ice and made a pot of tea. Each of the horses was given a nose-bag of oats. In less than an hour, we were refreshed and resumed our journey.

Both Craig and I were in pretty good condition. Walking that first day didn't bother me until about four o'clock in the afternoon.

45

Paul Nester in cap with three other travelers
in Cordova, Alaska.

Paul Nester with Genevive Redmond, Amy Hostler
and others at Tofty, Alaska, Spring, 1918.

Then I started to tire. Soon, however, I got my second wind and was able to keep up. We arrived at the Willow Creek roadhouse about seven o'clock that evening. We had traveled 25 miles that first day.

Roadhouses on the Fairbanks-Chitna trail were located about twenty to forty miles apart. They tried to locate each at the end of a good day's travel. Most were fairly large cabins constructed with logs. Some had one or more cabins adjoining. The main cabin usually was the lobby, the kitchen and the dining area. This is where the travelers congregated. In one of the other adjoining cabins was the bunkhouse. A huge stove was in its center and was surrounded with high drying racks.

That first night, after arriving, I was tired and hungry. After washing up, we all went in and sat down to a very fine meal. The cooks at these roadhouses were all superior. I think they each must have strived for the reputation of being the best cook. The more you ate, the better they liked it. Each meal cost one dollar and many times I have heard that if you didn't have the dollar . . . you ate anyway.

The care of your feet while on the trail in Alaska is a very important matter. Before going to bed, you always wash not only your feet but your socks as well . . . at least the inside and outside pairs. If you don't, you take the chance of winding up with frozen feet. Besides the three pairs of woolen socks you wear, there is what they call a California sock. It's a piece of burlap, about 18 inches square, that's folded over the socks. It acts as an insulator, absorbs moisture and helps keep the other socks clean. The California socks are also washed every night and they're all hung on the drying racks to dry. That first night, it didn't take me long to do my chores and get in my bunk.

Next morning, we were up at five o'clock.

After a "whopper" of a breakfast, we were on our way. Just before noon, we stopped at what I was told was one of the earliest settlements along that route. Cooper Center consisted of half a dozen cabins. There, we had a fine lunch.

In the afternoon, the going got slower . . . the grade became steeper. That evening, arriving at the roadhouse at Gulkana, I was told we had made thirty miles. For the next several days, each day, the going got a little tougher. In spite of that, we made nearly thirty miles daily. Sourdough and Meiers Lodge, each in their turn, came and went. Then we really started climbing! Twenty miles was all we could make that day. Between Huffmans and Paxtons, we crossed over the summit. What an experience that was! The next day, we made over thirty miles. By now, Craig and I had hardened up our muscles and were in good shape. We felt capable of facing up to any experience that might lie before us. From that day on, our daily mileage increased upward to over forty miles in a day. McCullum, Rapids, Delta, Richardson and Hardings, all came and went until we finally arrived at Fairbanks. We had accomplished three hundred and sixty miles in just over ten days.

We had been very fortunate on our trip to Fairbanks . . . the only new snow that had fallen was prior to our first day of travel out of Chitna. By the end of the second day, we had made our way through the new fallen snow and the going became easier . . . the horses appreciated this as much as we did. As we traveled high in the mountains, the trail went over glacier areas. It was here where I learned how spikes were put on the horses and why . . . to keep them from slipping on the ice.

Another very important thing I learned was how to cope with water springs which would build up pressure under the ice, then

48

burst, flooding the nearby area. If you happened along shortly after this occurred, the ice could be of most any thickness. Suppose it was thin. How would you know until after you broke through? Say the water was a foot or two deep? You're in trouble . . . get out fast as possible. If you don't . . . you freeze fast!

Fairbanks is located in the Tanana River Valley, near the very center of Alaska. It was the main supply base for Interior Alaska and had been selected to be the Northern Terminus of the Alaskan Railroad. It was not the northern construction center, however, that prize went to Nenana, sixty miles down the Tanana River.

In 1917, the population of Fairbanks was about six hundred. Most of the buildings (outside the business district) were log cabins. Utilities were delivered in a way I had never seen before. Along the streets, in what would be curbing areas, was a long box-like affair which contained water, steam and gas pipes, and electric cables. They were all packed and insulated to protect from freezing. The arrangement woked well.

After we arrived in town, one of the first things Craig and I did was to contact my uncle, Jake Howell. He was glad we came when we did. He was leaving the next morning for Nenana and would take us along.

The trip to Nenana took two days. For the most part, it was good going through flat country. Jake had his own double-ender with a full load of supplies. Both Craig and I got to take turns driving and, at the stops, I cared for the horse.

In 1915, Congress had appropriated money for the construction of the Alaskan Railroad. Nenana was fortunate . . . it was just a small river village, but was well located. It was selected for the northern construction center. Nenana had come a long way in the past year

49

Woodchopper, Alaska.

or so. Many key buildings had already been constructed and work on the right of way south towards Anchorage would start as soon as the snow melted. Hundreds of workmen had gathered, waiting for the chance to start work. Once the ice went out, Nenana was all set to burst forth with activity. That might be just one reason why the "Big Gamble" on the time 'The Ice Goes Out' started there. The Big Gamble is what Nenana is noted for today.

Craig and I parted in Nenana. Jake had been able to arrange a job for Craig in a local lumber mill. Next morning Jake and I took off for Woodchopper, a mine near Tofty, one hundred thirty miles further northwest. I drove the double-ender and took care of the horse for the entire trip. It took us four days, stopping overnight at Minto, Tolavana and Hot Springs.

If we had continued on down the river from Hot Springs, for another forty miles or so, we would have arrived at Tanana.

In those days, Tanana, was sometimes called Fort Gibbon and was located strategically at the confluence of the Tanana and the Yukon rivers. It was on the north shore of the Yukon. At this point, the Tanana river was one half mile wide and the Yukon was well over a mile in width. Fort Gibbon, headquarters for the United States Army Signal Corps for the interior of Alaska, was located there. The Signal Corps, in addition to its military duties, was responsible for the operation of the telegraph system throughout Alaska.

In 1917, communication was quite different than it is today. At that time, by sea, there was the wireless. Over land, for short distances, the telephone. For long distances, however, telegraph was the only way. The U.S. Army's Signal Corps had supervised the construction and the operation of the telegraph system throughout Alaska. They had built a very satisfactory system connecting most of the

51

important towns and larger villages. Even Hot Springs had a small telegraph station with three signal corp personnel. These small stations were necessary every fifty miles or so, just to keep the system working. Without the army and its signal corp telegraph operators, Alaska would have been isolated from the States.

Our destination was Tofty and the mine at Woodchopper, just thirty miles off to the north. Woodchopper had been a deep placer operation. Howell and Cleveland had mined the gravels from depths of thirty to fifty feet there. Operations had continued throughout the year. Gravel mined during the winter was hauled to the surface and piled until it could be sluiced in the summer. After seven years, the rich values gave out. Now the buildings were needed at Boulder Creek, twelve miles away.

Boulder was a hydraulic operation, much different from what Woodchopper had been. Work at Boulder was all on the surface. The gold-bearing gravels were shallow, nothing deeper than thirty feet. The gold was recovered by sluicing. Mrs. Cleveland, a very friendly and motherly-type lady, was in charge.

My first job was to help tear down some of the larger buildings for transfer to Boulder. I then helped in the moving and rebuilding. When that was completed, we built sluice boxes and riffles, cleared land, ground - sluiced cuts, arranged the sluice boxes and laid hydraulic pipe. That kept us busy until well into May.

One day, before the snow was all gone, Mrs. Cleveland asked me to take the double-ender to Hot Springs and pick up a load of freight. She also suggested that I take my mosquito net along . . . it was time for those "pests" to be coming out. Hot Springs, over thirty miles away, would take two days for the round trip. Snow was still everywhere and in some places it was quite deep. In the afternoons there was a lot of slush as it melted.

Fourth of July, 1917 at Tofty, Alaska.

I wanted to avoid as much of that as possible, so I made arrangements to start very early the next morning.

Early, the next morning, I was riding along enjoying the scenery. I had already gone over one third of the way. Climbing slowly up a mountain grade, I came over the crest and saw something off to my right about two hundred yards, I stopped. The horse apparently didn't see what I saw. Three cubs and a mother black bear were playing. Thank goodness, there was a fair breeze and it was blowing in the right direction. They were climbing up and sliding down a steep hill, just like a group of children! I watched them for, perhaps, ten minutes. Then, whispered a silent "giddy-ap" and cracked the reins. My horse never did see the bears . . . or smell them either! Guess it was one of my lucky days!

Early in the afternoon, I approached Hot Springs. From a distance I could tell something was seriously wrong. It looked like the whole area had become flooded with water! Tops of cabins were all you could see save the UPPER HALF of the General Merchandise store and that was a fairly new two-story building. On a hill adjacent to where Hot Springs used to be, I saw tents and some people. Then I saw a boat make it's way from the store building to the shore near the tents.

When the road ran into the water, I stopped. I made my way to a fairly high clearing I had spotted and tied the horse. Walking through the brush and woods, I made my way to where the people were camped. About a dozen folks, the full population of Hot Springs (so they told me), were there. This count included the three soldiers from the U.S. Army Signal Corps, who were stationed at Hot Springs. Their station too, was under water!

The day before, the ice in the Tanana River had gone out. They thought there had been an ice jam on the river nearby which caused the water to back up and come down through the slough (where Hot Springs was located) and flood their village. Fortunately, no one was hurt. Some of the men had saved the motor boat, a poling boat and a rowboat. With these, they were able to make trips back and forth for supplies. They were all in good spirits . . . happy that they had come out of it with their lives.

I inquired about the supplies I had come to pick up. Except for being eight feet under water, they were okay. No one had any idea how long it would take for the water to subside. I figured the best thing for me to do was return to the mine. I offered to take anyone who wanted to go back with me, but I had no takers. They all would wait it out where they were until they could resume their normal way of life.

I returned to the double-ender, unhitched the horse and gave him a good bag of oats. Returning to the tent camp, I visited, swapped stories, I had a good meal and rested until about midnight. Even then, it wasn't quite dark, so I hitched up and headed back to the mine.

The news I brought caused considerable excitement at Tofty. They wouldn't even let me pay for the meal I had there. On my way to Boulder the mosquitos that I had heard so much about, appeared just as Mrs. Cleveland had predicted! They came suddenly, in gigantic numbers. I don't know what I would have done if I hadn't had my head-net. Thank goodness, in that part of the country, the mosquito trouble lasted only about three weeks. The no-see-um gnats that came in the fall bothered me more than the mosquitos did.

When I arrived at Boulder I went through the same performance I had experienced at Tofty (relating the flood at Hot Springs). As

The bear I took care of and wrestled with, and his former caretaker.

soon as possible, I made my way to the bunkhouse and, in a very short time, was fast asleep.

Next morning the foreman, Herman Nichols, put me on a job that I kept for over a month. The ditch bringing water for the sluicing operation was just over five miles long and my job was to patrol this ditch and keep it in condition. With the melting snow and the rain showers of May and June, it was necessary to watch it pretty closely. One round trip a day, building up the weaker spots along the dike, kept the water flowing in the proper channel. I enjoyed that job and didn't get lonely at it. Finally, the snow was gone and the rain slacked off . . . that job was finished.

One of the other jobs I had been given right after my arrival at Boulder was the job of "Bear Keeper!" A year before, an Indian had brought a baby black bear cub to the mine at Woodchopper and left it as a mascot. That bear was now a yearling and just my size. I volunteered to take care of him.

The bear was secured on a thirty foot chain which slid back and forth on a cable between two trees that were about sixty feet apart. He was active and had a great time. I fed him and wrestled with him . . . we became great friends . . . or so I thought. One day, I was cleaning up his grounds. It was a mess . . . old sacks, all kinds of rubbish. I didn't know he was so attached to these "playthings." I had my arms full and was taking them away. Suddenly, from the rear, he jumped me! He hit me on my left shoulder and arm, laying open my shirt and my flesh about a foot! I swung 'round, bashed him in the nose and left . . . FAST! When I was out of his range, I took a look. There he was, flat on his tummy, with his head on the ground covering his nose with both front paws. If I hadn't been so mad, I would have felt sorry for him. Knowing Mrs.

Cleveland had a first aid kit, I went to her and had my wound cauterized. Thank goodness it wasn't deep.

Then . . . back to the bull gang at the mine. Moving pipe lines and sluice boxes, clearing land, ground-sluicing trenches, sledging boulders, doing anything and everything that needed to be done around a mine for ten hours a day . . . each and every day, except the Fourth of July . . . everything was shut down that day.

Tofty had quite a celebration on that Fourth: foot races, sack races, high and running jumps, three-legged races and a tug-of-war. There was a barbacue with all anyone could eat and, in the evening, a dance with nine women and about ninety-nine men. Boy was I lucky! Only one family in that entire area had a daughter. Amy was just fifteen years old and it was she who taught me how to dance.

Not long after this Fourth of July, I received a telegram. It was sent from Whitehorse, Yukon Territory. It said that my father would be on the river boat, Tanana, when it arrived at Hot Springs later that week. I showed Mrs. Cleveland the wire and arranged time off to meet my father and bring him back to the mine. When I saw Dad . . . I was shocked! Somewhere along the line, something he had eaten had given him ptomaine poisoning. Even though he was riding horseback, it was a tough trip for him from Hot Springs to Boulder. I felt so sorry, but knew I could do nothing.

Dad had come all the way from Portland to see me and to find out how I was doing when he had this bad luck. He was only able to stay a few days. With the next boat out, he was on his way. Dad didn't think much of Alaska and I have always believed it was because of this bad luck (ptomaine poisoning).

One day at lunch, the fellows got talking

about going fishing. Little Boulder Creek was just over the mountain about eight miles north. Two men especially wanted to go and they asked me along. I explained I had no fishing gear. They assured me there would be no need for that, they had plenty. We left after supper that night. It took nearly four hours to hike over the mountain to Little Boulder Creek. I found out what they had in mind. Besides the lunches they had in a sack, there were several sticks of dynamite, some caps and fuse. It took just a half stick of dynamite set off in a deep pool to get all the grayling we needed for a big fish fry back at the mine. We ate our lunch and headed back, arriving just in time for breakfast. After eating, we put in our second ten hour day of work. That was the first and last time I ever went fishing in that way.

Along about the first of September, it started freezing at night. This caused a water shortage and the mine eventually had to shut down. All the employees were paid off in time to take the last boat heading Outside. Most of the crew would be on that boat. There was a scheduled stop at Hot Springs, September 10th. Since I decided to stay in for the winter, I would take the last boat going up the river to Fairbanks.

Arriving at Hot Springs, I met two of the soldiers I had seen during the flood at the General Store. They took me to their station where the third soldier was on duty. We visited a spell, then one of them asked if I knew anything about a canoe. When I told them yes, I was invited to go on a duck hunt. Since my boat for Fairbanks would not be coming in until the next day, I accepted. I was told the soldier on duty had a shotgun that I could borrow . . . I didn't own one. They explained the plan: I would take the canoe and silently lead through the twists and turns of the slough. The noisy rowboat would follow at a distance. By taking the lead, I would be able to spot the birds in time to signal those in the rowboat. From that point on, they could use their oars as paddles (quietly) and we would all be able to get some shots.

In short order, we were ready to go. It felt good to be in a canoe, paddling again. My lead was about 100 yards. After three quarters of an hour or so, as I was slowly rounding a bend, I saw a huge flock of ducks, sitting huddled on the water. I back-paddled then swiftly turned, raising the paddle to signal my friends. In my excitement, I over-balanced and could feel the canoe starting to turn over! Through my mind, the thought flashed: "That man's gun!" I sprang out of the canoe, hoping to save it from turning over. All the ducks who had been sitting in the water were airborne in a moment! It must have been a strange sight for those boys coming along in the rowboat. When I surfaced, the canoe was floating high and dry, just as I had hoped. I knew the borrowed gun would be safe and that's all that really mattered. In just a few minutes, I was picked up. As we made our way back to the station, I was able to keep fairly warm by rowing . . . towing the canoe. I heaved a sigh of relief when I returned the shotgun to its owner.

After supper that evening, one of the workmen at the lodge asked if I would like to take another boat ride . . . this time in a motor boat. Naturally, I went along. We made our way out of the slough, down the river a couple of miles to a rocky point where a fish wheel was located. My friend started up the wheel and we watched it operate for a few minutes. Satisfied, he started the motor boat and we returned to Hot Springs. I was given an invitation to go with him again in the morning to see how the fish wheel was doing.

The next morning, after breakfast, we

started out. This time, however, we towed a large square-ended poling boat. I asked why he was towing that boat and he answered, "You'll see."

As we pulled alongside the wheel, it appeared to be sinking. There were fish boxes on each side of the wheel three feet by ten feet by three feet deep. Those boxes were loaded with salmon. As the wheel turned, it was picking up even more salmon and depositing them on top of the heap in the boxes. Some of them slid off the stack back into the water making their escape. The wheel was stopped and the poling boat was maneuvered alongside. With a throwing hook, my friend started transferring the salmon into the poling boat. There was an extra hook, so I got into the act. On occasion, a choice male would be spotted and tossed into a separate compartment. These were "choice" fish for the lodge and to be sent to Tofty and the mines. Fresh salmon for anyone headed that way. When the boxes were empty, we started back but this time, we pulled into a small cove where there was an Indian camp alongside a series of drying racks. We pulled up alongside. A group of Indians, mostly squaws and children, came to greet us and immediately started to work unloading the fish. Some of the Indians started to clean and hang the salmon on drying racks. They were not just for human consumption but were for dogs as well. This is how they put up one of the most important foods in Alaska.

CHAPTER 4

WINTER IN ALASKA

1917 - 1918

It was September, 1917. I had finished my first summer's work in the placer mines of interior Alaska. Now, I was on a river boat in the Tanana River on my way to Fairbanks. The boat was like many on the Willamette and Columbia rivers. The main deck was for freight and housed the engines. Two upper decks were for passengers and the boat's officers. The pilot house was located up on top. It was a good day's run with a short stop at Nenana. After a summer of hard work . . . this ride was great.

Our boat turned into the Chena River, a tributary of the Tanana, just below Fairbanks. The freight sheds and docking facilities are on the Chena. There were not many passengers going to Fairbanks . . . travelers at that late date were headed Outside. I was staying because I wanted to see Alaska through a whole winter . . . not just from March.

Registering at a hotel, I took a walk around town to see what I could recognize. It felt good just to be able to walk as far as you wanted. The change in the looks of a place from March until September in the north country is really something.

The last time I was in Fairbanks, everything was covered with snow and it was very cold. The only daylight we had was between nine in the morning and three in the afternoon. At other hours when you saw anyone on the streets, they were all bundled up so you could hardly recognize them until they talked . . . that is . . . unless you knew their clothing or how they dressed or walked. Now, the summer was about to end but Fairbanks looked like any other frontier town in the northwest. Instead of horse-drawn double-enders or dog teams, there were regular wagons and, on occasion, horsemen. In September, the weather was quite comfortable.

Next morning, I went down to the bank to cash my checks. I had been paid off with two. One was for $165.00 and the other $460.00. I told the teller to cash the small one and deposit the large one in a savings account. He examined them. They were drawn on the American Bank of Alaska. Then he handed them back to me and said, "The American Bank of Alaska is just down the street a block or so. If you take them down there, cash them and bring the money back here, I'll have your papers made out." That made me mad! I took both those checks to the American Bank of Alaska and transacted my business there.

That afternoon I spent over $75 for winter clothes and other things I needed. I passed an employment office and saw a sign, "Cook's Helper Wanted . . . Tungsten Mine . . . Good Pay." I inquired. They told me the mine had a good chance of operating for the next six weeks. I took the job.

Next day, I went to the mine with a wagonload of supplies. It was just a one day trip. The mine was a hard rock operation. The vein, on a forty-five degree angle, went to a depth of over 200 feet. Drilling with single and double jacks was necessary before charging and blasting. My job had nothing to do with that . . . I was the cook's helper and general handyman. There were twenty-eight men to feed. I set the tables, washed the dishes and helped do whatever the cook wanted done. In my spare time, I hitched up a horse and skidded timber into camp and cut it up with a power saw to fuel the cook house and the mill.

For about a week, everything went along fine. Then one day things really happened. The Chinese cook was a good one and I liked him but some people just don't like Chinamen. We had one of those . . . a big bully-type that made loud noises. I always set the table and this guy knew it. In preparation for breakfast, I would set the mush bowls up-side-down on the plates. Some prankster put an old dirty swab covered with iodine, under the bowl on "our" big bad man's plate. The first I knew of it was the ROAR he made . . . then the crash of the dish and bowl as it hit the wall over the cook's head! He started after the cook and that man took off fast! That's the last time I ever saw that poor Chinaman.

Later that day, the boss said to me, "As of NOW, you're the cook!" I tried to get him to change his mind, but he said until he could get a replacement, I was the cook!

I could take a lot . . . but that was the limit. Anyway, I kept busy, very busy, all through that day. In the afternoon, the supply wagon arrived back from Fairbanks. The driver brought bad news . . . the American Bank of Alaska had gone broke! Bank examiners had shut it down! My summer wages were gone! Now, I really had something to be concerned about.

My cooking job wasn't quite as bad as I expected. The Boss assigned one of the miners, an old prospector, to help me until a new cook arrived.

The crew still got quite a kick out of kidding me. They called me the "Chee-cha-co Kid." Every time I came up with something that didn't have a name, (like hash for instance) they called it the "Chee-cha-co's Mystery." After a week of this, a new cook finally arrived and I went back to my helper's job. My total time at the tungsten mine was just six weeks. The mill was forced to shut down because of extreme cold.

Returning to Fairbanks, I moved in with a friend who had rented a cabin for the winter. I would "batch" with him and share expenses.

A few days later, passing the same employment office, there was another sign: "General Helper on Drill." I didn't know what that was all about, but I was willing to try. They sent me out to Cleary Creek, where prospecting for gold was being done in deep gravels. The drill was a Key-Stone, powered by a steam engine. Usually they had a crew of five with the cook. The fireman and his wife, the cook, had quit. I took the fireman's place, cutting wood and melting snow for water needed in the boiler to keep steam up. I had never fired a steam engine before, but learned fast. Within a week, the driller's helper quit, too. The driller and I tried to carry on the work but it was just too cold . . . forty degrees below zero and we were living in a tent.

Back at Fairbanks, I was glad to have my friend with his cozy cabin. How great it felt just to be inside and warm. Most of those long dark days through December, after breakfast in the morning, we would walk downtown and spend our time around the card rooms in the hotels and saloons, watching the card players. I never played . . . didn't have the money to lose. I sure saw a lot of good poker and I found out who the winners were around that town. While we were doing that, we kept warm and also conserved our own wood supply. Usually, in the late afternoon, we would return to the cabin, cook up a good supper and then read until we fell asleep.

Shortly after arriving back in Fairbanks this time, I met my old friend Craig. He took me home to a very nice house and there, was my cousin Genevive. How we celebrated! Craig had a very successful summer at Nenana "contracting." He explained that shortly after going to work at the lumber mill, he found out that the city of Nenana was asking for bids on putting in the city's sewer system. Craig's engineering training came in handy. He did some figuring, submitted a bid and got the job. The work was completed before the freeze-up and he made a bundle! Craig and Genevive wanted me to stay with them. I didn't want to impose, but they insisted that I, at least, should come for the holidays and spend the week with them. I was very happy to accept.

This was the first Christmas I ever spent away from home. How wonderful it was to be with some of your loved ones. We enjoyed a turkey dinner with all the trimmings then talked and talked. Craig and Genevive each had some interesting experiences to tell and they got quite a kick out of some of mine. That day, passed so fast . . . it was great!

Displays in the store windows were most unusual that year. Congress had passed the new prohibition laws so all the liquor supplies in the stores, saloons and hotels had to be disposed of by midnight, December 31, 1917. If the liquor was not sold, it would be confiscated. You should have seen the bargain baskets with many bottles (a variety of fine liquors) for the price of ONE bottle. Guess it's a good thing I didn't hardly drink . . . at that time, even those few bucks I could not afford.

Then one evening Craig brought home the

NENANA ROUNDHOUSE FIRE

FIRE AVIATION

Fire of Unknown Origin, Destroyed Roundhouse At Nenana Today—Three Locomotives In Building At the Time—All May Be Total Loss—Watchman Not In the Structure At the Time; Fire Discovered By Watchman From Another Part of Town—Total Loss to Government Will Not Be Known Until the Locomotives Are Examined.

NENANA, Jan. 15—By far the most serious catastrophe yet experienced in Nenana was that which occurred this morning when fire, of unknown origin, destroyed the roundhouse of the government in the heart of the town. At the time were two big locomotives of the main line and one small switch engine, and, up to a late hour today, officials of the Alaska Engineering commission could not determine whether or not they would be useless for further use. The loss would not be far short of a late hour today could be put back in service they could be put back in to the commission. The total loss is estimated at $100,000.

...in another part of town, saw the blaze and turned in the alarm. Within a few minutes it was discovered that the fire was a bad one and the whole town turned out to assist in the work of fighting the blaze. The fire spread to the tank house and it, too, was destroyed joining and it, too, was destroyed.

Locomotives Damaged.

At this time the fire broke out there were three locomotives in the building two large main line engines and one switcher. All three were damaged somewhat, and up to a late hour nothing could be told to make a thorough examination of them, as they were so hot. It is a possibility that the men may be able to see that they can be used further.

NORFOLK, Jan. 15.— Walter Spoerman, German spy, wearing the uniform of the American army, was captured today, caught in the act of destroying a magazine of an army aviation plant. Papers on his person disclosed the fact that he had paid $90,000 to German spies working under the direction of Count von Bernstorff, formerly ambassador to the United States.

WILL BE SHOT

WASHINGTON, D.C. Jan. 15—A mass of evidence against Walter Spoerman is such as it shows that his operations have been such he will be shot as a spy. Until the present time it was considered a soldier of excellent character and well regarded by the officers who knew under whom he served.

There are no mitigating circumstances in the man's favor and it is said the war department is determined to hand out the extreme penalty when the guilt of suspected spies are proven.

RAID MADE OVER MORE BRITAIN

...out yesterday the Associated ...to disregard the ...and to observe ...tation as to ...morning, received ...Gunnison, the ...self-explana...

Jan. 14, 1918.

San Francisco suspended in the United States Food ...l food adminis-...rkless Satur-...and at least one ...fire.

...e this as far as ...NNISON ...for Alaska."

EATTLE ON ABROAD

daily newspaper. It was full of news about a large explosion and fire that had burned down the round-house at Nenana. Several train engines had been damaged. Right after I read the details, I got an idea . . . go to Nenana and get a job cleaning up the mess and putting the engines back in shape. That was all I needed. Early next morning, I was on my way to Nenana. It was only sixty miles and I knew the route . . . I had been over it before. This time, however, I was alone.

By late that afternoon, I made it to the Midway Roadhouse. That second day, I started in time so that I arrived at the railroad superintendent's office in Nenana that afternoon. When I hit him up for a job, he laughed at me. He asked, "What makes you think you could get a job here? There are hundreds of men just waiting around for things to open up in the spring." I told him why I needed the job and I blamed it all on the American Bank of Alaska . . . you know, he put me to work . . . on the clean up gang already cleaning up that mess.

I was assigned a place to sleep in a very nice government dormitory. Not only that, I had my meals at the commissary . . . boy, oh boy! How fancy that was compared to how I had been living earlier while working in the various mines. There was of course a difference in the wages. Mines paid $5 a day and you got your board. The government just paid $3.60, but it was a life-saver for me.

After about two weeks, we had that mess pretty well cleaned up. One day the Superintendent came by. He called me off to the side and asked me if I knew anything about firing a steam boiler. I was able to tell him "yes" . . . but I didn't tell him my experience totalled just a bit over a week. He then said the clean-up crew was finishing up that evening. Mechanics had been able to get one of the three damaged engines back in working order and that engine would be busy each day. At night, they needed a hostler to keep the fires going in the engine's fire box and sort of "baby-sit" that critter. Each morning, steam would have to be up, ready for that engine to go. Did I want that job? . . . HORRAY! Now I had a real job!

I was carefully instructed on just what I had to do. From that time on, I was excited about my work, cleaning, oiling and fussing around that engine. Then, I made a deal with the cook at the commissary. Instead of taking a lunch for my midnight meal, the cook would give me the makings . . . what wonderful midnight meals I had, cooked in the engine's fire box on a coal shovel. For the next couple of months, I was happy on my railroader's job.

Then one day, Jake Howell looked me up and asked me to help him. He had a team of heavy work horses that he had contracted out to haul in bridge timbers for the railroad. He needed someone he could depend upon to handle those horses, skidding in the timbers. He offered me $6 a day and board . . . plus . . . a job at the mine all summer at the same wages. I would have turned even that high offer down except I figured I owed him for giving me the chance to come to Alaska. I took the job.

Within a few days, I got a ride in the engine I had been taking care of, to a place they called Clear (for many years Clear has been the site of the largest U.S. military air base in Alaska) at the end of the tracks, about thirty miles away. There were just a few buildings: a cookhouse, a barn, a small bunk house and a foreman's shack. The caretaker and his wife, the cook, lived in the cook house. They were friendly people and the only ones there. I was told the team would arrive the next morning. The bunkhouse had eight bunks and a good stove . . . but the place was a mess. I spent the entire afternoon cleaning it since that is where I was going to live.

Next morning, the team arrived and I went to work yarding in the heavy timbers from nearby forests for the pile-driver. The timbers were cut and trimmed and the snow was just right for skidding them down the hill. My main difficulty was finding all of them under the snow. I had another problem as well. Just where were the skid-ways the loggers had cleared to get those timbers out? Some days I lost plenty of time just searching. My friend, the caretaker, helped me as much as he could and his wife, the cook, treated me like a son. They both made my job easier.

One day, the work train brought the pile-driver foreman and his crew of eight men. When I got in from work that night, that foreman told me, in very plain language, that I better get my stuff out of that bunkhouse . . . he needed it for his eight-man crew. I told him that I had cleaned that place up and that I wasn't moving . . . don't know why I did, because that man was six-foot-two and I was scared of him! Anyway, I stayed there that night with seven of his men . . . the eighth man had to sleep in the barn.

Next day, I went to work as usual, perhaps a bit early, to avoid him. That night at supper, the foreman told me, "If you don't have your stuff out of that bunkhouse by nine o'clock tonight, I'll come up there and throw it and you out." After I was through eating, I returned to the bunkhouse. I had a .25 caliber high powered rifle a Nenana friend had loaned me when he heard I was being transferred to Clear. That, he said was good moose country. I got the rifle out and spent the evening cleaning it and shining it up. The men saw that I had plenty shells but I never put one in the barrel . . . bluff was my only intention. The other men at the bunkhouse were friendly and there

70

was a feeling of expectancy in the air. One of them must have taken a message to the foreman cause he didn't show up . . . nothing happened.

For several days, my work went along as usual. Then, one evening, when I came in from work I met a new man who had arrived on the work train that day. He handed me a letter. It was from Jake Howell ordering me to turn the team of horses over and return to Nenana. He had another job for me.

Next morning, I helped the new driver with the harnessing and told him the ups and downs of the job. When the work train arrived, I was all packed and ready. As that train pulled out, I wished "Good Luck" to the man who was going to be sleeping in the barn.

It was now well into April. In a little over a month, the ice and snow would be going out fast. A lot of supplies had to be transported to Boulder, so I went back to the double-ender job. The trails were in great shape and the four-day run from Nenana was easy going. Most of my trips were short, though, just the one day jaunt from Boulder to Hot Springs.

Next thing you know, it was May and I was back on the same job I had just one year before . . . patroling the ditch. The run-off from the snow-melt could do serious damage in short order. Then too, those rains . . . but, in a few weeks, the slush was about gone and the rains nearly over.

I was back, working in the cut at Boulder. This time, however, I was working as a "giant" or "monitor" operator. The giant is a huge nozzle used in the mining industry. An 18 inch pipe from a penstock (a box regulating the flow of water) was gradually reduced down to the giant, which had a four inch nozzle. The force of water coming through was mighty powerful. You could tear away a twenty foot bank mighty fast. You had to be very careful with it.

Once every two weeks or so, when sluicing had been completed in one cut, the bull gang would have to change the pipe line and sluice box set-up to another cut. This would take several days. While they were making the change. I had another job. Mrs. Cleveland had taught me how to recover gold that got caught in the rough bedrock before it reached the sluice boxes. This usually occurred in a semi-circular area, out eight or ten feet from the mouth of the first sluice box. I would set up a small sluice box and work the bedrock. A clean-up would be made each noon and each evening before I left that box. My daily take would be between twelve and twenty ounces. One day, I brought in one nugget that weighed sixteen ounces!

That year, the Fourth of July was celebrated just like it was the year before. The only difference was that I knew a lot more people a lot better. I was no longer a 'Chee-cha-co.' This qualified me as a 'Sourdough.' Alaskan people are great and I was happy to be considered one.

At the celebration, I met a friend who I had worked with the year before. John Boulton told me about a sub-lease he had obtained on some of the tailings at Woodchopper. He explained that for years it had been necessary to put on an extra man with a heavy fork, to throw out heavy smooth rocks that blocked and interferred with the operation of riffles. A few years back, an inquisitive worker had one of those rocks assayed. It ran 40% to 50% tin. After pay dirt at Woodchopper ran out and the mine shut down, he obtained a lease on the tailings there and made a fortune! Because John was a friend, a sub-lease was obtained from him. John told me that he was recovering enough light gold (gold adhering to quartz or other light material) to pay for his operation.

The tin he recovered was pure profit. I wanted
to see that operation. So on my way back to
Boulder, I stopped by John's lease and was
shown the whole bit.

Oregon Journal

PORTLAND, OREGON, SUNDAY MORNING, OCTOBER 27, 1918

PRICE FIVE CENTS

THE WEATHER

343 LIVES LOST ON COAST

Socialists Will Insist on German Republic

KAISER'S Time Turned Back Sit Its Flight One

ALLIES TO Boat at 2 O'Clock This Sunday Morn

CUT LOOSE

FROM HIM

Summer Time Over and Up, elsewhere Gets Back Hour Stolen Away Last April.

GOES DOWN WITH 300 PEOPLE

Canadian Pacific

Great Battle of Hindenburg Line Means Victory

BY FRANK H. SIMONDS

Foch's Masterly Strategy in Coordinated Operations of Palestine, Bulgaria and Champagne, Rank Him Among Six Greatest Commanders and Master of Greatest Armies in Human History.

Germans Putting SHIP SLIPS
Up Better Fight FROM REEF
On Whole Front WITH ALL
Than For Weeks ON BOARD

CHAPTER 5

THANK YOU CHARLIE

1918

Back at Boulder, the time passed rapidly. Through July and August, nothing exciting really happened. Handling that giant had become so automatic that, as I worked, I day-dreamed a good part of each day.

One morning, about the first of September, I was dreaming away. In one more week, the mine would be closing down. If we worked just six more days, there would still be plenty time for the crew to catch the last boat out before freeze-up. Most all the crew would be going Outside. A few would remain to prospect and trap.

There was another very important thing to think about. the War had been going strong for some time. Many of the men had plans of enlisting in either the army or the navy . . . I'd go for the navy. On August 17th I had turned 18 years old, so by law, I had to register. When we stopped at Tanana, I could register there.

When I heard my name called, my thinking was jarred.

"Hello Paul!" I turned and recognized my good friend, Charlie Snellstrom. I hadn't seen him for about a year.

"Hello Charlie . . . it's good to see you. You look tired."

"I am . . . my outfit shut down last night. The packer's are taking my baggage to Hot Springs for me. I came by to pick you up."

"What do you mean, pick me up?"

"Well, you know how it is, Paul. You're the only one about my age around. I sure get tired listening to all the old Sourdoughs. I walked thirty miles out of my way to get you to quit your job and go Outside with me. The boat is due at Hot Springs at ten o'clock in the morning. We can make it."

"Why should I quit and go with you? I get six dollars a day for running this monitor and that's one buck more than you or I made last year!"

"Ah . . . come on Paul . . . have a heart. I need company.

"Charlie, I don't need company. When we shut down next week, I'll have sixteen men going out with me."

The dispute continued. Charlie hadn't walked thirty miles for nothing and he wouldn't take no for an answer! When the noon time relief arrived, Charlie and I went down to the mess hall. The outfit fed us well. Charlie knew some of the crew and I hoped he would give me a break and visit with them. But no! When I returned to work, he returned to work with me. From one o'clock until five o'clock we went over and over the reasons why I should or should not quit and go Outside with him.

Then, contrary to all arguments something suddenly came over me . . . "Go with Charlie!"

At six o'clock my shift came to an end. I went to Mrs. Cleveland and told her that I was leaving. She was shocked by such sudden notice and disappointed that I should leave when, in just one more week, the whole outfit would be closing down. After some discussion, however, she was agreeable. I drew my final pay check.

After Charlie and I had supper, I packed my things. Luckily I was able to borrow a pack horse to cart my luggage. We told our friends good-bye and by nine o'clock that night, we were on our way.

For Charlie, it was a tough pull. He had worked one day, walked all that night (thirty miles) and then he had spent the entire day on his feet talking to me and visiting with old friends. Now, without sleep, he was doing his second thirty miles.

Occassionsally, we would stop for short periods of rest. After we got over that first hard mountain stretch, the country was not difficult for traveling. Except for a few small rolling hills, the land was flat. In spite of the "no-see-um" gnats, I really enjoyed that trip.

At eight thirty in the morning, we arrived at the roadhouse at Hot Springs, tired and hungry. We cleaned up and had an excellent breakfast. I had just arranged for the return of the pack horse when we heard a shrill whistle. The river boat was about to dock at Hot Springs landing.

Charlie and I quickly made our way down to the boat and boarded. The purser informed us that we were lucky . . . we had been assigned the last available stateroom. In a short time, the boat was under way. There was a good current running and the channel was fairly deep and easy to follow.

Depositing our luggage in the stateroom, Charlie and I made a tour of the boat. We had just completed our tour when the call to lunch was sounded. The food was good and we ate heartily. Charlie excused himself to go to our stateroom for a nap . . . he was so tired.

I made my way to the pilot-house to see

the Captain. I hoped that the boat would be stopping at the city of Tanana long enough for me to go ashore and register for the draft. The Captain was a pleasant person and understood my problem. He said, "We'll be stopping for about two hours and if you hurry, I'll hold the boat for you."

When the boat docked at Tanana, it was late afternoon. I was one of the first off and headed directly to the fort. Within twenty minutes I was at the main office. I told the Captain in charge that I had come to register. He laughed, explaining that his "out-of-the-way post" hadn't received the instructions or the materials necessary for the required registrations. I must have looked worried because he quickly added that he would help me.

To my relief he gave me the following letter:

"To whom it may concern, Greetings:
This is to certify that Paul Nester, resident of Tanana, Alaska, home address Portland, Oregon, 216 Fremont St., being of the age of 18 years, did make application to this board for registration, as provided by the order of the President of the State of Oregon. Date of registration not being set for Alaska, this board could not register him.
Dated this 12th day of September, 1918.
(signed) Geo. G. Beim, Chairman.
Local Board #21   City of Tanana
Tanana Alaska."

I thanked him for the letter and hurrying back to the boat, I showed it to the Captain and thanked him for his help.

Soon, we were underway. Since we were headed up the Yukon in a north-easterly direction our speed diminished. This river was much wider and shallower than the Tanana and the channel was hard to follow. Because of this condition, there were two boatmen on the bow: one on the port and one on the starboard side. They would alternate using their sounding poles and calling the depths to the bridge. It was interesting to watch them work but I was tired, so I made my way to our stateroom and 'hit the hay.' Charlie was still asleep.

Early the next morning we were awakened by the boat's whistle and in a few minutes, the engine stopped. I looked out the porthole and saw that we were alongside the river bank near a heavily forested area. We dressed and went down on deck. Firewood was being carted aboard. The boilers used a lot of fuel and these wood-loading stops were made daily. This was a great day for the wood-choppers and their families. All year long they chopped and piled wood, waiting for the boats to arrive. Now their mail and provisions had arrived and this was their "payday!" It was time to celebrate . . . and a "Saturday night" atmosphere prevailed! It wasn't long until we were again underway.

The majority of passengers aboard were either miners or railroad workers. Because of my experience during the past winter working on the railroad, I enjoyed talking to both the railroaders and the mining people. Charlie also met some of his old mining friends, people who he had worked with before. He spent considerable time visiting with them and, for each of us, the time passed quickly.

Occasionally when we made a stop, either to load wood or at some riverside village, we would take on passengers. Since all the staterooms were taken, these people had to find a spot for themselves. In spite of this they were all friendly and happy to be aboard, on their way Outside. The cook excelled in his trade and the meals were always good . . . I think Charlie and I were his best customers! Even the crew was jovial and helpful. This boat, you see, had a good Captain.

Slowly, we made our way up the Yukon. A day or so after we passed Rampart, the river widened to several miles and the channel became hard to follow. Sand bars and shallow water slowed us down to barely a crawl. These conditions lasted for nearly a week. When we reached Fort Yukon, on the Arctic Circle, our heading changed. Now we were going south-east. Each day as the river became narrower, our speed increased. Finally, after ten days on that river, we reached Dawson, the center of mining in the Klondike and the largest town in Canada's Yukon Territory.

There we had a full day's stopover and everybody went ashore. There were many things to see, especially for one who had never been there before. Dawson was the center of activities during the Klondike gold strike of 1896. Thousands of "would-be" miners had arrived by 1898 and gold mining history was rapidly being made. Many stories were told about these first discoveries and I wanted to see where they happened!

A story that fascinated me most was the one about the Cheechaka (tenderfoot) who had just arrived from the states. He was green as grass. He believed that it would be easy to find gold anywhere. So he went to a saloon and ordered "A gold mine to make me rich!"

The bartender and the group at the bar seemed very sympathetic and understanding (ha ha). They escorted him out of the saloon to the middle of the road . . . pointed to a distant hill and said, "Go to the top of that hill and dig there." The Cheechaka went to the hill they had pointed to and started digging. Just as he expected, he discovered, staked, and eventually, operated one of the richest mines in the Klondike! This mine (which ran for many years) was known as the "Cheechaka Hill Mine."

Charlie and I didn't make it to the hill,

but we both enjoyed a drink in that very same saloon. We really hadn't quite finished when the boat's whistle sounded and we had to take off.

We were soon all aboard and leaving Dawson headed up a faster-flowing Yukon. Trees in the forests on each side of the river, spruce, fir, birch and tamerick, were taller. The scenery was becoming more and more beautiful.

One of the most exciting places we passed was Five Finger Rapids. The five fingers were made by five huge rocks (islands) set across the river like huge stepping stones. At this point, the current was very swift. As we approached what appeared to be the widest gap between two of these giant rocks, I was very apprehensive. The engine was doing its very best and it took fifteen minutes for the boat to travel its length as we made our way through this gap. When we were safely past that point and in reasonably safe water above the rapids, most everyone on the boat silently sighed, "Thank God, we made it."

We were fortunate in having fellow travellers aboard who were able to point out many of the overnight camping places. Little, Salmon, Eig, Lewis River, Thirty Mile, Lake Labarge and Squaw Rapids, were a few. Many of the names reflected the stories that were told about these places.

Finally, after nearly fifteen days on the Tanana and Yukon rivers, we arrived at Whitehorse. This was the upper terminus for the Yukon river boats. In the early days, this was one of the most exciting camps on the river and those fortunate enough to make it that far, celebrated. Many raced on to discover and stake a claim . . . they all were known as "stampeders."

In the late 1890's when word of the discovery of gold in the Klondike reached the states, thousands of these "Stampeders" left their homes and headed for the gold fields. Ocean liners took them north to Skagway. From there, they had to climb on foot over the high coastal mountain range, through either the White or the Chilkoot Pass. At the border crossing, they were stopped by the Royal Canadian Mounted Police and each person had to have at least one thousand pounds of supplies. From there they proceeded on to Lake Bennett where they camped and built their boats for the trip down the Yukon.

Many a "stampeder" has lost his boat, supplies and some have even lost their lives to these treacherous waters. The Whitehorse rapids were considered one of the worst. The first good camp site below these rapids was called the "drying out place," and eventually became the town of Whitehorse.

By seven o'clock the next morning, Charlie, most of the river boat passengers and I were aboard the "Skagway-bound" train departing Whitehorse. The White Pass and Yukon Railroad, a narrow gage line, had been constructed between 1898 and 1900. The train was made up of an early-day steam locomotive, coal car, baggage car and six early American-style coaches. Each coach was furnished with a pot-bellied stove and a coal box and the ride was quite comfortable.

The scenery along this route was spectacular! Snow capped mountains, glaciers, beautiful lakes and forests with steep grades and trestles across very deep canyons. At Carcross, the train stopped to pick up several more passengers and, by noon, we arrived at Lake Bennett, our lunch stop. A very fine meal had been prepared. Moose-steak, potatoes and apple pie! We relished every bit of it.

After eating, we had time to see a log church which had been built about the year 1898 by the early "Stampeders." During the winter months, after completing their boats, there was nothing to do but wait for the break-up of ice and the coming of spring. Somebody had a good idea . . . why not build a church? So, they all went to work. What a church they built and to this day, it stands.

Leaving Bennett, we headed for Skagway arriving about five o'clock. Charlie and I got a room at the Golden North Hotel, a three story building with a gold 'Arabian-styled' dome.

Skagway is the seaport terminus located at the north end of the Lynn Canal which is also the north end of the Alaskan Inside water passage. In the early days, most all supplies for Alaska's Interior passed through this port. The gold and other mineral products came out the same way. Skagway, indeed, was a major port. It also had the reputation of being the wildest town in Alaska!

One of Skagway's main tourist attractions was its cemetery. The most conspicious grave in that cemetery was Jefferson "Soapy" Smith's. He was an ambitious gambler, a good organizer and an "out-and-out" crook. He had arrived in Skagway early enough to either own or control the saloons, cat-houses and a good percentage of the other businesses in town. He even tried to get his hands on the financing and control of the White Pass and Yukon Railroad. Those people, however, would have nothing to do with him. There had always been opposition to Soapy and to his ways of operating. But Soapy organized and got himself officially appointed captain of Company A in the Alaska National Guard.

Then came the 1899 Fourth of July celebration! Skagway had never experienced such a day! There was a parade, brass bands, floats, and of course, Company A. In the evening there were fireworks, both the Fourth of July kind and those triggered by the confrontation between Soapy's organization and the Railroad people. Soapy was challenged by one of his adversaries. He was the first to fire a shot! . . . other shots followed! When it was all over, several, including Soapy Smith were dead! Soapy is long gone, but his grave remains a major tourist attraction at Skagway.

Early the next morning, the Outside travelers were aboard the Princess Sophia, when it pulled out from Skagway, south-bound. This ship was built in Glasgow, Scotland, in 1912. She was an oil burner, 245 feet long with a 44 foot beam, constructed to carry passengers. Captain Louis P. Locke, in the service of the Canadian Pacific, commanded this ship on its Vancouver/Victoria/Skagway run.

For the first hundred miles or so, we traveled south on the Lynn Canal, between towering mainland mountains. These mountains, for the most part, were covered with snow. Gigantic forests made a "road" down to the sea. We were quite fortunate as the weather was ideal through the entire trip. We passed glaciers and watched huge masses of ice break off and fall into the sea, making a tremendous thunderlike noise. This was a common occurrence at this time of year.

We made short stops at Juneau, Wrangle, Ketchikan and Prince Rupert but due to the time schedule, the passengers were allowed to go ashore at Juneau only.

After three days on the Princess Sophia, we arrived in Victoria. Here we transferred to a Washington State ferry for a short run through the San Juan Islands before arriving in Seattle . . . we were Outside at last!

We stayed in Seattle that night and early the next morning took the train to Portland, arriving that afternoon. Charlie and I had enjoyed a great trip together. He would be going on to southern Oregon on the same train so now it was time to say "good-bye." We would, however, see each other in the future. At that time, I had no idea of the great favor

Charlie had done for me . . . and I wouldn't know until a week from Sunday morning.

Leaving my luggage at the depot, I walked up to the street-car stop on the Steel Bridge and took the William's Avenue car home. What a welcome I received when I walked in and surprised my Mother and Father! My brothers and sister arrived home from school and joined in the joy of this happy day. After eighteen months (nearly to the day), here I was . . . home and happy!

For the next ten days or so, I just took it easy. One day, I went to the U.S. Navy Recruiting office to enlist. When they asked for my registration card, I told them that I didn't have one, but showed them the letter I had received at Fort Gibbon. I was informed that, according to their rules, they couldn't enlist anyone who did not have a registration card. The lieutenant told me where I could obtain one . . . this I did. However, I didn't go back to the recruiting office that afternoon.

Early Sunday morning, my father awakened me. I dressed and went downstairs and Dad had the "Sunday Oregonian" spread out on the kitchen table. In very large print across the top of the front page was this startling message:

PRINCESS SOPHIA SINKS - 343 PERISH
ALL ON BOARD LOST IN ALASKA WATERS
DISASTER REGARDED AS WORST IN MARINE
HISTORY ON PACIFIC COAST
SHIP RUNS ON REEF IN BLINDING
SNOWSTORM. SLIPS FROM REEF WITH
ALL ABOARD

Shocked, I read all that had been written about that disaster. To my great sorrow, I found the names of my friends . . . those who I had worked with all through the summer! I thought of Charlie. If it had not been for him .

. . . my very good friend . . . my name, too, would have been on that list . . . <u>THANK</u> <u>YOU</u> CHARLIE!

ALASKA

CANADA

NOME

YUKON RIVER

TANANA

TANANA RIVER

FAIRBANKS

FORT YUKON

DAWSON

MOUNT McKINLEY

ANCHORAGE

Chitna

VALDEZ

CORDOVA

Whitehorse

SKAGWAY

JUNEAU

Gulf of Alaska

YUKON RIVER

BOULDER CR.

TANANA

TOFTY

WOOD CHOPPER

CHARLIES MINE

TANANA RIVER

HOT SPRINGS

CHAPTER 6

UNITED STATES MERCHANT MARINE

1918 –1920

Since returning from Alaska, visiting my family and just relaxing at home, had taken up most of my time. It was good to be able to visit some of my old friends.

One day, I met a former High School classmate, George Russell. He had just returned from a trip to England and had signed on a ship as a crew member in the Merchant Marine.

We swapped stories. When he found out that I was about to join the Navy and I had experience firing steam boilers and engines, he didn't like that idea one bit. He said, "Don't be silly . . . the Merchant Service pays twice as much as the Navy and they are desperate for help. Besides, you'd see more of the world in one year with the Merchant Service than you would in one whole hitch in the Navy."

Before that week was over, George took me down to the "Firemen, Oilers and Watertenders Union" and introduced me to the secretary. After inquiring a bit to satisfy himself, the secretary asked me if I had $15.00 (the union membership fee). I gave him the money and he wrote out a work order (as an oiler) to be delivered to the First Assistant Engineer on the U.S.S. Bellbrook. It was a brand new wooden ship that was taking on cargo at St. Helens.

Then he instructed me, "When you arrive at the ship, before you deliver this work order, take a look at the ship's engine. If it looks like an electric motor, you've got it made . . . it's a turbine. But if it looks like the insides of a gasoline car motor, it's a reciprocating engine and God Help You! Whatever it is, tell the engineer that the last job you worked on was the Opposite of what he said! . . . By the way, do you have a passport? You can get one at the Federal Building. Then, take this work order to the Bellbrook. It's due to finish loading shortly and will be getting underway." Extending his hand, he added, "Good Luck."

I thanked him and George and I went to the Federal Building. Getting my passport was no trouble . . . it just took time. At St. Helens, I located my ship and went aboard. I took a look down the engine room hatchway and was relieved to see that engine was a turbine.

Finding the First Assistant Engineer, I gave him my work order and followed the secretary's instructions in answering his questions. He appeared satisfied and asked if I had brought my baggage aboard. When I said "No," I received permission to get my luggage and report aboard early the next morning . . . ready to go.

Telling my parents was one job I dreaded . . . they didn't want me to leave . . . so many of my pals had been leaving in the past year or so. That evening passed so fast . . . visiting, packing and telling about the ship I would be working on.

Next morning, I reported aboard and was shown to my quarters. Three oilers occupied a

Paul Nester, Crew Member.

S.S. Bellbrook, one of the wooden ships
built on the Willamette River during the War.

small but adequate room amidship. It was close to the galley, the petty officer's mess and the engine room where I would be working.

That first day, I was assigned to work with the Third Assistant Engineer. Mr. Cobb's duties, while in port, were the upkeep and repair of all auxillary machinery on the ship: pumps, winches, generators, ice-machines, etc. He informed me that I would also be working with him while at sea. We would have the midnight to four a.m. and noon until four p.m. sea-watch.

That evening, I became acquainted with the other two oilers. One was very friendly and we hit it off well together. Canby worked with the First Assistant and helped him keep the turbine in good working order. The other oiler worked with the Second Assistant. Their responsibility was to keep the boilers in the fire-room in condition.

By now, the seriousness of my job was commencing to get me down. I didn't know a thing about all that machinery or just what my duties would be. That night thinking about it, I lost plenty sleep.

Next day after lunch, I had an opportunity to talk to Canby alone. I confessed how ignorant I was about the engine room and asked for his help. He grinned saying, "I didn't think you knew too much and I am glad you told me . . . now, we can do something about it. There's a good chance we will be pulling out tonight . . . probably on my eight to midnight watch. You'll be relieving me at midnight, so why don't you come down early . . . say, about ten o'clock? You can make the rounds with me and I'll give you a quick short course on "How to be an oiler."

What a break! My luck hadn't run out after all! The Bellbrook pulled out early that evening and headed down the Columbia. I stayed on deck enjoying the sites until it was time to go below.

When I finally went below, Canby was expecting me and we started making a round. We checked gages, felt bearings, oiling where necessary and carefully inspecting each machine. We checked and oiled bearings the complete length of the shaft alley. Returning to the engine control area, we had completed one round. Underway, a round was made every twenty minutes. Then I was told that any signal coming from the bridge, over the control telegraph, had to be answered. It was my duty to answer then log the exact time and what the signal was. Half Ahead ⌐, Full Ahead ⌐ , Stop / , Full Astern ∨ , or whatever. Then, while the engineer was busy with the throttle, it was up to me to turn on or off any other machine that needed attention. When maneuvering, there's more than plenty to do!

Canby only explained and showed me the important duties in order to get me through the first watch. Very soon, it was time to call the relieving watch. First we awoke the engineer, then the watertender, the firemen and coal-passers. After returning to the engine room, we made one more round.

At midnight, Mr. Cobb took over from the First Assistant. Then Canby and his engineer departed. Now, I was on my own, I was responsible. The first few rounds I made, I was excited. Soon, however, I got the hang of it and the time flew by rapidly. Everything went okay. First thing I knew, it was 3:40 a.m. and time to call the next watch. I had been told to always call the oiler first. That way, he could get down to the engine room, make a round and then, if there was anything wrong that they did not want to take responsibility for, inform his engineer. Four o'clock, I went off duty and straight to my bunk and a well earned sleep.

I awoke in time for breakfast and had a good one. Going on deck, I enjoyed watching

91

the scenery along the lower Columbia for an hour or two. I returned to my bunk took a nap and woke up in time to get an early lunch. Before twelve o'clock, I was down in the engine room . . . ready to start my second watch.

This time, Canby stayed over and accompanied me on my first round. He told me more about what each machine did and about the controls. I sure appreciated his help. Everything went smoothly the first part of that watch . . . then, all of a sudden, that ship started to bounce, jump and twist . . . it was getting hard to keep my balance without holding onto something. Mr. Cobb casually remarked, "I've never seen this Columbia River Bar behave." It's surprising how much you can tell, just by feel. He was always busy at the throttle during times like this, when the going was rough. Then I got that "funny" feeling in my stomach. I headed for the bilges in the shaft alley. There, I was out of sight. My next few rounds were made quickly . . . then . . . back to the shaft alley. I was sure glad when I was relieved at four o'clock. That night I skipped my supper and hit the hay. That's all I needed . . . just a bit of rest and I was back on my feet again. The Columbia Bar was passed and so was my sea-sickness. Never again, during my life, have I been sea-sick.

Our ship was headed for the Panama Canal, coasting south-easterly down by Oregon and California. At times it was clear enough to see land. Most of the time, however, the weather wouldn't permit. I believe we saw more of Lower California . . . we had clear weather off that coast. Then, off the Central American coastline, we encountered a North-Easterly Storm. It lasted for days. The ship bucked like a cayuse and, in order to maintain our south-easterly heading, we had to steer nearly south.

When on watch, during stormy weather,

Entrance to the Panama Canal.

Watertender, Mr. Cobb, and myself.

Unloading coal at Malta.

the engineer spends his entire time at the throttle . . . it's a tough job . . . reacting to the feel of the ship, shutting down every time the stern is about to go out of the water and opening up as the bow goes into the air . . . you learn by feel. If you make a mistake and the propeller comes out of the water, the vibration is terrible. Everyone aboard ship knows you made a "boo-boo."

By the time the storm was over, we had been at sea for sixteen days. Our coal bunkers were practically empty and we still had one full day's travel before the closest coaling station. Our Captain wired for a tug. When our ship arrived at Panama, it was at the end of a long cable . . . under tow!

Panama City is an interesting port. To the south, it faces the great Panama Gulf which has a very large and deep harbor. Canby and I got a lucky break. While the ship was taking on coal, we got time off, hired a cab and saw the town. The historic places and buildings were great tourist attractions. For me, the most interesting points were the water-front. The small boat harbor where local trading boats were unloaded and their cargoes marketed: bananas, coconuts, all kinds of tropical fruits as well as other produce. It was interesting to watch.

The Panama Canal had only been in operation for a few years and our trip was quite educational. Electric "mules" hook on and tow the ship into and out of each of the locks. Going through Calebra Cut, we passed the largest crane in the world . . . took pictures. The crane was clearing away a massive slide that had slowed down traffic. Gatum Lake was created by building dams and flooding large forested areas. For many miles, the tops of trees could be seen sticking out of the water, bordering the sides of the channel.

The Canal is 44 miles long and about 100

yards wide. It's series of locks takes you well above 100 feet over sea level. It was hard for me to believe until I checked on the map, but traveling from the Pacific to the Atlantic, you go in a north-westerly direction. It took us nine hours to pass through.

I was told Colon and Christobal, ports on the Atlantic side, were great historical places. Nearby, both Columbus and Drake made history. Our stay at Colon was short . . . we took on supplies, water, etc. . . . then we were on our way north-easterly up through the Caribbean.

Our first stop was at Port au Prince, Haiti. I never did find out why we put in there. It was only a very short stop, long enough to pick up a stowaway.

Three days out from Port au Prince, as we traveled towards the Azores, there appeared on deck a very skinny, small colored boy, about 14 or 15 years old. He had made his way aboard and hid in one of the life-boats. He finally got so hungry and scared, he came out. His face looked as much green grey as black. Poor kid, he was scared to death and half starved. The Captain detailed him to the galley, under the cook's care and in short order, that brought about a fast cure and a very happy colored boy.

Our next stop was at the Azores. Nine islands, all Portugese, made up the group. They are located about two-thirds of the way across the Atlantic. The best harbor was at Horta, on the island of Fiail. A collier, anchored in the harbor, was considered an emergency coaling station. Ships needing coal would tie up alongside and fill their bunkers. There were other ships ahead of us, anchored in the bay, awaiting their turn.

We anchored out about one quarter of a mile from shore. One of the seamen was detailed to handle the work-boat and transport shore-bound crewmen back and forth. First opportunity I had I went ashore.

Hortia was just a small town, built on hilly land. The houses were primarily two stories. They all had balconies and were painted in attractive colors. Nearly every road away from the water-front and from the business section was narrow and paved with cobble stones. Walking to the edge of town, I came to vineyards and orange groves. Not far from town, on high cliffs overlooking the sea, lookouts were posted to watch for whales. (Whaling is very important to the people of the Azores). Further on, a few miles up the hill, was a volcano crater with a lake at the bottom. All along the volcanic countryside with its green cultivated areas, the scenery was beautiful.

At the edge of town, in a residential section, I passed a milkman, driving a herd of goats. He delivered "on the hoof" and milked his goats right in front of his customers' house . . . they knew they were getting their milk fresh!

Many sailors, coming back to the ship, from shore-leave, brought a bottle or two of liquor with them. Our seaman, manning the work-boat, had sampled quite a few of these bottles. He was young, big and had a powerful voice. He loved to sing and sang as he rowed. I had walked a long ways that day so I turned in early and went right to sleep. I was awakened by a loud crashing sound and a shrill scream! Jumping up, I ran to the deck just in time to see Mr. Cobb throw a life-preserver overboard. The work boat was hanging vertically from one line connected to a boat davit. Someone on the bridge brought the searchlight beam down to sweep the water. Then from out there somewhere in the darkness, came a powerful voice:

I'm forever blowing bubbles
Pretty bubbles in the air,
They fly so high, nearly reach the sky,
Then like my dreams, they fade and die.

Fortune's always hiding, I've looked everywhere.
I'm forever blowing bubbles, pretty bubbles
                                        in the air.

There was no doubt about whose voice that
was . . . the searchlight spotted him with his
head inside the circle of the life buoy, happily
singing away. By this time, the current had
carried him abreast the stern but the line on
the life-buoy was holding. A Jacob's-ladder was
lowered over the side near the stern. Our
friend was able to maneuver over to it and
climb back aboard. He explained, "I tried to
lower that work-boat by myself, but it got away
from me. I intended to go ashore and buy my
own bottle."

While we were taking on coal from the
collier, I watched some of their crew fishing
and catching devilfish. The fish were taken off
the hook and repeatedly slammed onto the deck.
I soon found out why. Octopus, like abalone,
have to be tenderized. When the cook had
finished with those devilfish, the chowder was
delicious.

As we pulled away from the collier, we left
our little colored stowaway behind. He was to
be put aboard some other ship headed for Port
au Prince.

From the Azores to the Straights of Dover,
was about a week's run . . . at least it was for
us. The first half of the way was fine, but
then we came into heavy fog. Our speed was
reduced to half ahead. After the first 24 hours
of this, life on watch really became tough. On
one 4 hour watch, I recorded 42 signals from
the bridge. From Half Ahead to Full Speed
Astern then Stop . . . Slow Ahead . . . Half

Ahead . . . Full Speed Astern then Stop . . . over and over. We had a hard time keeping up with the things we had to do in the engine room. We were wondering, "What was happening on the bridge? Who was going Nuts?" We finally found out . . . it was the Captain. Poor man, he wouldn't turn over responsibility to any of the mates and leave the bridge. He'd had no sleep . . . guess he was just "going off his rocker." This was his first ship as a Captain and he had been a good one. Navigation was perfect and in spite of the fog, we hit Dover right on the nose. As we headed up into the North Sea, the fog lifted. One day later, we arrived at our destination, Hull, England.

Hull, located at the mouth of the Humber River, was the third largest port in England. Like many European ports, in order to make a harbor, dams were built to hold back the river waters. Gates on those dams would only be opened at high tide to let the boats in and out and there were docks for many miles.

Besides its general import and export, Hull harbor was the central base for a very large fishing fleet. During the War, it had been a major sea base for U.S. Navy Destroyers. Next to London, it ranked highest as a target for German bombers.

We were there, unloading, for nearly a week and awaiting a new Captain to take over command of our ship. Our regular in-port eight hour day-watches replaced the sea-watches. As usual, I was on with Mr. Cobb. Evenings, we could go ashore. We were advised however, to go in groups of four or more. We were told that Hull was not too healthy a place for American seaman going ashore alone.

I, of course, had to find out for myself. I met a girl and we took in a show. When I took her home, just before we arrived at her house, we passed a pub on the corner of her cul-de-sac street. Several fellows were standing

98

out in front. My girl friend said, "When you come back by here (and you have to because, there's no other way), watch out for those fellows . . . they don't like Americans."

When I approached the group had increased to six. As I got closer, they leisurely moved out, spacing themselves at intervals to block the street. I picked one man (not quite as large as the others) and started to jaywalk in his direction. About twenty feet before I reached him, I rocketed into a fast run, socking him hard as I flew by! For the next three blocks or more, you should have seen that chase . . . I, of course came out number one! I felt that I had the most to lose . . . in case I lost!

Later, back at the ship, I was filled in as to why such a thing was happening.

All American sailors like English girls . . . . the girls would turn down most any Englishman just to go out with a Yank. It started to be dangerous. Just before we had arrived, many Yanks got badly beat up. When the Destroyer Force departed Hull, the Officer in charge gave liberty to every possible sailor, with specific orders to go ashore in groups of six or more, to remember what had happened to their friends who traveled alone and to return just before high tide. That's when the fleet would be leaving for the last time. In Hull that night, there was close to a massacre of the Limies. Especially those hanging around the pubs. Excited sailors talked about that fracus for months.

We finally finished unloading our cargo and departed Hull. This time, with a new English Captain, an old maritime man who knew his business. Our ship headed back through the Straights of Dover, rounded the south end of England, then headed north through the Irish Sea to Cardiff, Wales.

Wales lies on the west side of England,

facing the Irish Sea. It runs from Liverpool Bay on the north about 130 miles south to Dee Estuary. Cardiff is its largest city and is located on the south coast. Our ship took on a full load of coal, coal mining being their chief industry.

I well remember the fish and chips shops at Cardiff. You could get all the fish and French fried potatoes you could eat for only six pence! It was delivered to you folded in an old newspaper and you could eat as you walked. That was very good food and those shops did so much business, I wondered if anybody cooked or ate at home.

How different the Welch people were. Ashore in the evenings, as you walked the streets, it was impossible to get out of range of groups of singers. They loved to sing and were marvelous.

My grandfather, Howell, was a Welshman so I studied the ancestral history of the Welsh and got a good answer to my question: "Why do the Welsh like to sing?" It seems that in the 13th Century, when Wales was over-run by the British, they discovered that the Welsh had no written language . . . but they had wonderful memories. Many a Welshman could name his ancestry way back to the time of Christ. The English even with his knowledge of writing could barely do this. In Wales, in order to inherit property, the people had to trace their ancestry back many generations. Because of this, they formed the habit of singing the names of their people back as far as their memory permitted. It became a pleasant past-time . . . so that's why the Welsh people love to sing.

Our ship headed south from Wales, crossed the Bay of Biscay and coasted along past Spain and Portugal. When we reached Gibraltar, we took a left turn through the gate, heading easterly on the Mediterranean.

It was a mighty big change from the cold of January in the north . . . so nice and warm . . . the water so blue and calm. To our starboard, we passed Morocco, Algeria and Tunisia. We dropped anchor about one half mile off shore at Malta, just off the capitol port of Valletta. It was necessary to await inspection by the port authorities and our turn at the docks.

It was four o'clock in the afternoon and I had just come off my afternoon shift. As was my habit, I went on deck for a breather and a look. What I saw was fascinating! The anchor was barely down when a fleet of bum-boats surrounded our ship. These small boats were loaded with a variety of merchandise. In short order, the floating salesmen were making their pitch. The "English" they used was hard to understand but their efforts were paying off. It was the best show I had seen for a long time. Before I realized, it was supper time and I hadn't yet washed up. Returning to my quarters, I found my friend, Canby, (the oiler I had relieved at twelve o'clock).

"Paul, how'd you like to go ashore?"

"Sure, but how?"

"Some of the guys have made a deal with one of the bum-boat men to come back after dark and pick them up under the poop deck. They invited me to go along and there's room for you, too. They say its a fair sized boat and it'll bring us back at midnight . . . how about it?

"But, Canby, how about your eight to midnight watch? . . . and what about my twelve to four a.m. watch?"

"The rumor is, Paul, that at six o'clock we go off sea watches and go on port watches, (eight on and sixteen off)."

"Fine! Let's go see the sights and have some fun for a change!"

I didn't want to think what might happen

if I got caught jumping ship in some foreign port . . . even for a few hours.

Canby and I had our supper and returning to our quarters, we started getting ready for our adventure ashore. One of the sailors, the one who had invited Canby, appeared at the door.

"I've got bad news for you, Canby . . . I got it straight from the horse's mouth. They're not going on port watches until eight o'clock in the morning and you have to work the eight to twelve watch."

That's a tough break for me, but Paul can still go. He relieves me and if he's not back by midnight, I'll just stay on for him . . . but that'll cost you a bottle of Johnny Walker, Paul."

A short time later, a small boat made its way silently (in the dark) to a position under the poop deck and a Jacob's ladder was lowered over the side. Six sailors and one member of the black gang (those who work below deck) silently made their way down to the boat. Casting off, the current swiftly carried us away from the ship. The motor was started after we were some distance away. Soon we were approaching a landing area. Before docking however, the boatman demanded his fee . . . and it was plenty steep! He told us he would meet us at midnight for the return trip. This business concluded, we headed for town.

Merchantmen have a thing going between the deck hands and the black gang. This would be similar to a group of U.S. sailors and marines or vice versa. Being the only member of the black gang on this expedition, I had been catching hell and didn't appreciate it one bit! When the group headed for one particular district, I had a feeling there would be trouble. I got lost.

I made my way into the town. Walked up and down the streets and as I walked, I began to think of the chance I was taking. What would happen if I were picked up . . . a foreign sailor off a ship that was still in quarantine? So far, I had been able to avoid talking to anybody. But now I had to take the chance. After all, I had made a promise to Canby. I entered a bar and was able to purchase a bottle of Johnny Walker with no difficulty . . . even though I had no local money. Accomplishing this, I felt it was time to head back to the meeting place. Once there, I found an inconspicuous spot to wait. Eleven thirty p.m. . . . twelve midnight . . . twelve thirty a.m. . . . one a.m. . . . nobody showed up! Suppose the sailors had come back to our meeting place early and been picked up by the boatman? Suppose they had returned to the ship without me? Right quick, I started making my way up current, along the shoreline. The moon had come out almost full and the light on the bay was beautiful . . . my ship sparkled in the moonlight. What a mistake I had made by leaving her? A pretty fair breeze had come up and the nice, smooth Mediterranean was not so smooth any more. I had traveled well over an hour when I came upon an area I had been searching for . . . a fisherman's harbor.

I made my way until I spotted what I had been looking for . . . a small rowboat tied alongside a floating dock. The oars were lying on the bottom under the seats. I untied the boat, sizing up the wind direction . . . thank goodness, it was blowing towards the ship like the current was running. I gave the boat a powerful shove into the current and hopped aboard. Seating myself, I reached for the oars. They didn't budge! . . . They were padlocked to the bottom of the boat! The boat, already out some 100 yards from shore, was moving fast! As quickly as I could, I started to work placing my hands together and using them as a paddle. I leaned first over one side on the boat and then the other and headed towards my ship. As a boy, I had done this with a canoe on the Willamette River. It is most effective. . . if you can work hard and fast enough. Believe me, the beautiful Mediterranean can kick up quite a chop at times and in short order, I had worked up a good sweat!

I was approaching my ship head on, going at a pretty good clip. I grabbed the anchor chain, carefully secured the rowboat and shinnied up the chain with Canby's Johnny Walker in my back pocket. Climbing over the rail, I silently made my way to my quarters. No one was there. It was 3:50 AM and the third oiler had gone down to the engine room to relieve me.

In just a few minutes, Canby came up. He was delighted to find me safely back. I told him my story, gave him his whiskey and we each had a drink and turned in. I had just fallen to sleep when I was awakened by Canby's sailor friend. He was relieved to learn that I had been able to get back OK. He told how he and the others had returned to the meeting place after I had left. They, too, waited and finally decided our bum-boat man had become alarmed and had never returned for any of us. They had made their way, just as I had, along the waterfront. Fortunately, they found a fisherman who was just preparing to cast off on an early trip. He couldn't refuse the money they offered to get them to the ship. When they came aboard . . . it was starting to get light . . . what a night!

Later that morning, the harbor patrol came by with the port authorities. The row boat I had used had been discovered tied to the anchor chain. To say it created a commotion aboard, would be putting it mildly. That day all six of those sailors, one at a time, contacted me and told me what they thought of me for leaving the rowboat tied to the anchor chain . .

104

. it didn't bother me in the least. The fisherman got his boat back and nobody squealed.

The Maltese Archipelago consists of three main islands: Malta, Gazo and Comino. They are located 50 miles south of Sicily and 220 miles north of Tripoli in the middle of the Mediterranean. Malta has sheltered harbors and was considered a most valuable military location. A coaling station was located there, also. Since before the Copper and Bronze Ages, 6000 years ago, people have made these islands their homes. Phoenician, Greek, Roman, Arab, Norman, Spanish, Italian, French and British people have at one time or another, occupied and ruled this prize location. The language spoken is Maltese and English. The religion is Catholic.

The islands are made up primarily of limestone. There are numerous temples, caves, caverns and catacombs below the surface. Ancient underground temples, with priceless relics of past centuries, have been discovered . . . some go down several levels. Limestone was the building material used by ancient as well as modern builders.

Valletta was constructed in the 13th Century. Its buildings are architectually beautiful and the street layout is splendid. People there are industrious. They have to import nearly 80% of their food. The merchants appear to be pushy . . . but they really aren't . . . even though they stand outside the entrances of their stores and beg you to come in and buy something. Really, they are friendly and do have bargains. The women create delicate lacework and beautify many articles that can be purchased at a reasonable price.

The coal docks were most unusual. Probably, their regular bunkers were full, so we unloaded our full cargo into an open coal yard . . . there wasn't even a dock there.

Several barges were strung out and walkways arranged from ship to shore across them. That entire shipload of coal was carried off in baskets on the heads of men and boys and deposited 150 yards away from the ship. I took pictures which I still have.

Leaving Malta, we headed west back across the Mediterranean. We passed through Gibraltar and followed the Spanish coastline northwest until we came to the mouth of the Huelva River. We anchored in the harbor off the port of Huelva, close to the border of Portugal. It is south of Merida and west of Sevilla. We would pick up a cargo of copper ore there and again, we had to await our turn loading.

It was too warm a sunday afternoon to have to spend anchored in the harbor. Sundays, there's no work (except that which is vital). So . . . we went swimming, most of the crew, that is. When the tide runs, the Huelva river has a strong current. We would go to the forecastle, dive off, take one or mabe two strokes and be almost midship. There, a boom had been rigged with hanging lines, so that you could latch onto them, pull yourself over to the ship's steps and climb back on deck. It was fun and just right for a hot afternoon.

I had just come up the steps when I heard our chief mate hail one of the galleyhands. Some of the crew had been drinking and the mate thought that one young fellow had too much. The mate told him to go back to his quarters and change out of his swim suit. The galleyhand left. Five minutes or so later, we heard a yell, "SO, YOU THINK I CAN'T SWIM, DO YOU?" We all turned in time to see him make a nice dive off the poop deck. The mate, our singing sailor, and another seaman took off after him in our work-boat . . . fast! The current was carrying him out into the Atlantic ocean. Two and a half hours later, the work-boat returned with the galleyhand rowing.

By this time, he was very sober and very very tired.

In those days Spain was having disturbing problems. A condition, bordering on revolution, was haunting the authorities. Communists were blamed and laws had been passed in an effort to control these problems. One of the laws passed was that no foreign sailor was allowed to go ashore in Spain. I can't understand why I felt the way I did, but I resented that law.

In a day or two, our turn came and we moved into the loading docks. As in Malta, bum-boats came alongside, selling merchandise to the crew. I found that, for a reasonable fee, one could arrange to go ashore. However . . . no one would agree to bring you back. I found myself trying to figure out a way to get back when and if I was able to get ashore. Two Spanish soldiers were on guard at the gang plank, checking every one coming on or going off the ship. A third soldier walked back and forth on the warf adjacent to the ship. As far as I could see, the soldiers didn't pay any attention to the upper deck of the pier, where the ore cars were or to the conveyor. Occasionally, a train would bring ore cars out onto the upper deck of the warf. The ore was dumped into a hopper then fed into a conveyor which took and dumped it into the ship's hold. At one point, the conveyor was only about 15 feet above the ship's deck. One could drop down onto the deck without any trouble.

I had been quite friendly with one of the sailors and when I told him my plan, he thought it was great . . . he wanted to go along. I needed the company, so we made a deal with one of the bum-boat men. Early that evening, we were ashore. Before it got dark, I was able to take some pictures. Neither of us realized beforehand how we, as foreigners, stood out. We were glad to see it get dark. We avoided the public places and main parts of town as well as we could. What we saw most of was the outlaying areas. Finally, about ten o'clock, we started to head back. A train of ore cars came by and we hopped aboard. It was the copper ore train that brought cargo for our ship and we were able to ride to a spot very near the loading hopper. Slowly and carefully, we made our way out on the conveyor and when in position we dropped to the deck. Nobody saw us and our shipmates wouldn't believe we had been ashore. Later, when we arrived in Liverpool, we got our film developed and the pictures turned out good. Only then did they believe.

It wasn't long before the ship's holds were filled, the hatches battoned down and we were underway. We left that sunny, warm, part of the world and headed north to Liverpool, the second largest port in all of England. This was another one of those harbors made possible by building dams and gates at the mouths of rivers or bays . . . holding back the waters which entered with the high tides.

When Canby and I found out that it would take nearly a week to unload our cargo, we made arrangements for shore-leave. It took several hours to travel to London by train. The trains looked funny but they traveled very fast . . . so different from ours in the United States.

London, the Capital of England, is located near the mouth of the Thames River. It is one of the main trading centers of the world and has one of the largest ports, with docking areas for over 500 ships. It, too, was created by building dams and gates and holding back the high tides (like Hull and Liverpool).

London has several hundred hotels. Crosby and I chose one near Trafalger Square. Admiral Nelson, the man honored for the early 1800's defeat of Napoleon's French Fleet and the Spanish Fleet combined, is honored by a monument in the center of his square. A short distance down the Mall, past St. James Castle and Park, alongside Hyde Park is Buckingham Palace, the home of the Queen. That's where tourists see the changing of the Guard.

Our trouble was which ones do you choose to see, when you only have four or five days to see all the sights? . . . London Bridge, St. Paul's Cathedral, Westminister Abbey and directly across the Thames, the House of Parliment? There are hundreds of museums and galleries, numerous theatres and many symphony orchestras. Places like Piccadilly Circus, Palaces, Castles . . . you name it . . . it's there for you to see!

The time passed so fast . . . we had no more started sightseeing than our time was up. We had to return to Liverpool and get back to work.

Our next port of call was Swansey, Wales, where we took on another cargo of coal. We headed back to the Azores and dropped anchor in the harbor off Faial Island. This time, we took our turn operating as an "emergency" coaling station. Traffic was heavy and we unloaded fast . . . sometimes having a ship on each side of us. Thank goodness, it didn't take long to empty our holds, then back to England.

The day before Declaration Day, we dropped anchor off the Bill of Portland on the south coast of England. This was the place where Portland Cement was first invented. Limestone was ground with clay and heated in a blast furnace. The result was cement to make concrete which helps build the great structures we have today.

Declaration Day dawned a most beautiful day. We had to celebrate! The sailors challenged the black gang (of which I was a member) to a sail boat race. Two of the small work boats could be rigged for sailing. We accepted the challenge, but there weren't many

109

Washington, D.C., 1919.

Ore loading pier at Huelva, Spain.

sailing sailors in the black gang. They couldn't find anyone with much experience, so they chose me. For a crew member, I picked one of the firemen who had some sailing experience on the Willamette. Although we lost, we had a lot of fun!

That afternoon, we were, again, challenged. This time it was a baseball game on the beach. I was on that team, too. This time we didn't lose but I sprained my ankle when I stepped into a hole! I was in a bad way for a week or more.

The crew of the Bellbrook had signed Nine Month Shipping Articles and our time was nearly up. We were awaiting new orders and when they came we proceeded on to Fowey, a small port in an estuary on the west side of Wales. There we loaded a type of moulding clay used in glass manufacturing. This material was used often for ballast. It was far better crossing the Atlantic with cargo than without. In about two weeks, we dropped anchor in Hampton Rhodes at the mouth of the Chesapeake Bay. There, most of the crew was paid off. We were put ashore, bag and baggage at Norfolk, Virginia, with transportation money back to Portland, Oregon.

Canby and I decided that since we were so close, we should go see Washington, D.C. We took a passenger boat up the Chesapeake and then up the Potomac River. As we passed Alexandria, Virginia, we noticed a shipyard with a brand new ship at its dock. It looked like the ship was just being outfitted. Both Canby and I thought it worthwhile to check to see if jobs might be available . . . after we finished seeing sights in Washington, of course.

For an American who has never seen our Capital, Washington D.C. . . . it's quite a place! It was first planned by George Washington but he picked Major Pierre C. L'Enfant, a French engineer, to design the

Capital. It proved to be a good choice. Just think . . . laying out a 160 foot wide boulevard (Pennsylvania Avenue) between the White House and the Capital Building . . . what an imagination!

During the first several days, Canby and I were able to see the White House, the Capital Building, the Washington Monument, Arlington National Cemetery and some parts of the enormous National Gallery of Art.

One day Canby suggested we go down to Alexandria and see if, by chance, we might get jobs on the new ship we had seen at Alexandria. Soon after this suggestion was made . . . we were on our way.

Reaching the ship, we went aboard and sought out the First Assistant Engineer. He asked how we happened to come along just when they were planning to pull out (the next day). As it was, they needed oilers who could also do the water-tending. Canby assured him we could do the job . . . I, however, wasn't so sure . . . anyway, we signed Shipping Articles for a trip to Europe.

The ship, the Anna E. Morse, was a much larger ship than the Bellbrook. There were three Scotch Marine boilers which were fired with oil instead of coal and powered by a 2000 horse power triple expansion engine. That job, oiling along with the watertending, would be a challenge for me. Good old Canby had come through once more. He also gave me a short, but adequate, course on "WHAT" to do and "HOW" to do it.

Next day, we were headed down the Potomac. When we came to the Chesapeake we turned north and went up to Baltimore. There we took on general cargo. Later, we proceeded on to Delaware Bay and Philadelphia where we completed the loading.

Philadelphia was our nation's first capital, the place where Freedom was established in the new world. How I would have enjoyed seeing that town! . . . but there wasn't enough time. Our ship was loaded and we had to pull out.

While the ship had been making these short trips, I stood several watches and had learned how fortunate I was getting my first job on the Bellbrook with its turbine. That reciprocating engine, with its huge crankshaft making 50 to 60 revolutions per minute was something! . . . The oiler has to feel the revolving con-rod bearings as they turn to see that they are not overheating. It takes a bit of doing, but I managed. The most difficult thing for me to learn was the operation of the water-injector. Getting the water into the boilers against that enormous pressure was one thing I had difficulty learning.

Good, it was summer and the trip across the Atlantic was pleasant. This new ship was twice the size of the Bellbrook and the quarters were much more spacious. The operation of its engine, however, with its auxillary machinery, kept me a lot busier than I had been before. Time passed quickly . . . the first thing I knew, we were bouncing around in the Bay of Biscay off the coast of France. We docked at St. Nazaire which is located at the mouth of the Lorie River, southwest by west from Paris.

Unloading the cargo started. The way the stevedores worked, it looked like we wouldn't be there very long. That evening I went ashore.

I went into a tailor shop I spotted in downtown St. Nazaire. For some time I had been in need of a new suit. One of the salesmen who spoke good English sold me the material and tried hard to also get the job of tailoring. I didn't feel the ship would be in port long enough, so I turned him down and took the material aboard with me that evening.

The next day we found out our ship would be there for nearly a week. That evening, with the new cloth under my arm, I headed for the tailor shop. I didn't get far before two French plain clothes men picked me up and took me to their police station! Apparently, they thought I was trying to smuggle the material ashore. They didn't speak English . . . I couldn't speak French! . . . no one there could speak English . . . not a word I said was understood! After what seemed to be an eternity, I spotted a French-English dictionary on a shelf. I wrote out in French, "Come with me and I will show you where I bought this cloth." They accompanied me to the tailor shop and, thank goodness, the same salesman was there, He made the necessary explanation and after many apologies and a few kisses on each cheek (* -- ! ? ! -- *) the French policemen released me and took off. By the time the tailor finished measuring me for my suit, the whole evening was shot.

St. Nazaire is noted for its shipbuilding. Some of the finest and largest passenger ships ever to sail the seas have been built in its shipyards. I believe the S.S. Normandy was one.

I had gone ashore one evening, with one of my sailor friends. We wandered about for several hours just taking in the sights. Having worked up an appetite, we went into a cafe for a bite and a drink. A small orchestra was playing and their music was good. Then they played "The Stars and Stripes Forever," . . . my friend and I felt pretty good about that! He took a tip to the orchestra and on his return to our table, a big colored man stood in the isle and blocked his way. This colored man proceeded to cuss him, the United States, and all it stood for. The next thing I knew, I was in the middle of a firstclass "free-for-all!" Apparently . . . everyone took sides. Except for the colored man and the group of colored people he was with, I couldn't tell friend from foe. I was able finally to make my way close to my friend. I yelled "Let's get out of here" and, as we made our exit a French Police squad arrived, swords drawn. The last we saw of that fight, the police were walloping those still fighting with the flat sides of their swords. Our timing was perfect and we headed back to the ship without further delay.

It only took a few days to unload our cargo. We then headed out to the Dover Straights and on up into the North Sea. One day, while on duty, I had just completed making a round and was standing at the foot of the engine room ladder talking to the engineer. Our wiper was doing his clean-up job and was working near one of the boilers. He accidentally struck the water glass gage with one of his tools and it exploded. Steam gushed forth making an escaping hiss! That Wiper took off . . . fast!

It was just a half dozen steps through the steam to reach the pull chain to shut off the steam to the water glass. When I did that and got a chance to look, the poor Wiper was up three flights and still traveling . . . fast! The engineer and I enjoyed a good laugh. Our destination was Antwerp, Belgium, sixty miles up the Scheldt River. A terminal of the Albert Canal, Antwerp was noted for its trans-shipment efficiency. Being a very busy port, we had to anchor out and await our turn at the dock. As usual, a work-boat was put to work transporting sailors going to and coming from shore.

Belgium people are friendly. Canby and I enjoyed our first visit to the city of Antwerp. We were both upset and felt badly however, over a crazy incident for which one of our own countryman was responsible.

After an evening of enjoying the sights of Antwerp and its hospitality, we hired a hack to take us back to the Siberian Docks, near where our ship was anchored. We were well on our way when the hack was hailed by two sailors who also wanted to go to the Siberian Docks. Since there was room, Canby and I agreed it was okay if they paid their half for the ride. That, too, was all right with the driver. As we traveled along, I formed the opinion that the class of New Yorkers they were, was to New York what the Cockney is to London. They had been drinking and so had we. When we arrived at the docks, Canby and I paid the driver our half of the fare and when we left, those fellows were still arguing with the driver. Canby and I walked to a point near our ship and called for the work-boat. It was perhaps 15 minutes before it arrived. We climbed down the sea-wall ladder ten feet or so, got into our boat and headed for the ship. We had gone only a short distance when the two fellows we had been riding with appeared on the sea wall and started calling us all kinds of names! This burnt us up. The sailor turned the work-boat around and headed back to the sea wall. Canby happened to be in the bow and started climbing the ladder. From the stern, I could see he was just about to be kicked in the head. I yelled, "Watch it Canby!" just as the kick was made. Canby was able to dodge but still caught a glancing blow on one ear. He backed down a bit as I grabbed an oar from the seaman. When I swung the oar, the fellow jumped back. Canby went over the top and after him . . . fast! I climbed the ladder and when I overtook them, Canby had him down. I looked for the other New Yorker but he was nowhere to be seen. I returned to find Canby holding his victims ears, bumping his head on the cobblestones. I put my hand on Canby's back and got him to stop . . . we left the fellow there . . . unconscious!

Before one week was up, the cargo for Belgium had been unloaded and we had taken on another for New York. Soon we were on our way, back across the Atlantic. The Anna E. Morse was fast and made better time going than it had coming.

As we approached the east coast and came in sight of land, there were many ships in view, going in all directions. I felt peculiar excitement stirring within me. We went through the Narrows and came in view of the Statue of Liberty . . . what a grand sight! Glistening green copper, standing over 300 feet high . . . holding the torch in her right hand! What a wonderful symbol for freedom and liberty! Thanks to all those French people who worked so hard to get the funds for her: a gift from them to celebrate our first centennial . . . and thanks to Frederic G. Eiffel, the designer, whose Eiffel Tower in Paris is proof of his ability for such a task.

The Statue of Liberty is located on Liberty Island, about one and a half miles southwest of Battery Park. We went past and anchored just above Jersey City.

My first day ashore, I took the subway at the Battery to go up town. The train traveled so fast that, first thing you know, I was way out in the suburbs. To return to downtown New York, I took one of those double-decker busses and rode on the top deck . . . what better way to see the sights? I went all the way down to Wall Street in the financial district. This is where the New Amsterdam Colony was first settled.

Manhattan, the piece of property the Dutch purchased from the Indians back in 1626 for twenty-five dollars worth of trinkets, was quite a buy! The Colonists settled and worked the land then lost it to the English in 1664. About a century later, they were able to take it back . . . what a deal!

Our next "move" was to Philadelphia. We had completed the contract in our Shipping

Articles so both Canby and I decided it was about time we went home. We drew our pay and gave ourselves one full day to see the sights.

Philadelphia, the city of "Brotherly Love," was founded by William Penn. It became the greatest city of freedom in all of North America. Our Nation's first Capital, it was where the Constitution was written and where the home of Benjamin Franklin, who did so much to shape our nation's history, was. No wonder our Liberty Bell is located there.

It took four days to cross the continent and return to our home and our starting place, Portland, Oregon.

U.S.S. Vestal, Repair Ship for the Pacific Fleet, 1921-1923.

CHAPTER 7

UNITED STATES NAVY

1920 – 1923

I enjoyed being back home again very much. Visiting with my family and friends, the time passed quickly. Portland was quiet and peaceful . . . the War had now been over for more than a year. All the shipyards had shut down and most of the other businesses and shops had returned to normal. So many young men, recently discharged from the military service, were still looking for work. It didn't take me long to come to the conclusion, that it wouldn't be easy to find any kind of a job here.

With nothing much else to do, I dreamed about one of my favorite places, Alaska. I had never heard of a "bush pilot" but that's just what I dreamed about. What a wonderful thing it would be to be able to furnish air transportation to the interior of Alaska. Many times, even before I left that country, I had the same dream. If only I knew how to fly!

One day when I was downtown, I passed by the Post Office at the Federal Building. There I spotted a Navy Recruiting Poster. The words "Join the Navy . . . Learn to Fly" appealed to me. I went into the recruiting office and asked many questions.

When they found out that I had served in the Merchant Service as an oiler and watertender, they really wanted me. I was told that they had a Machinist Mates' School at Great Lakes Naval Training Station where Aviation mechanics were trained. If a student did well, they could go on to learn about flying. Because of my Merchant Marine experience, they offered me a rating . . . if I would enlist. I signed up for three years, starting at the Great Lakes Aviation Machinist Mates School.

When I told my parents and the rest of the family what I had done, they didn't like it at all! But by that time, it was too late to do anything about it.

Several days after I enlisted, I boarded a train, traveling the North Pacific route to Chicago. Winter was beginning and when we made a short stop at Glacier National Park it was plenty cold. At Chicago, no time was lost as we transferred to a north-bound train that took us on to our destination.

The Naval Training Station at Great Lakes is one of the largest operated by the Navy. It is located on the west shore of Lake Michigan, about thirty miles north of Chicago. Many schools, each teaching a different craft for the training of Navy petty officers, are located there.

My first several days were spent taking physical examinations and undergoing tests to check educational background. I was vaccinated eleven times over a period of about three months. Then, I was outfitted and assigned to a school company.

For me, military life was no big deal. I had already experienced the service in the Oregon National Guard and knew just about what to expect. In addition to six or eight hours of school classes each day, considerable drilling was done.

The subjects we studied at first were basic: math, mechanical drawing, blue prints and work in the shops chisling, chipping, filing and fitting. Later, we studied metals and blacksmithing. We learned how to operate many different kinds of machines from the most simple grinders, drills and shapers to complex milling machines. It was all very interesting.

That winter, quartered in those old wooden barracks it was cold. The wind off Lake Michigan was frigid. Every few weeks a trainload of coal would pull in and all available gobs (gobs are to the Navy what the G.I. is to the Army) would turn out in dungarees to unload the coal and fill the steam plant bunkers.

When Christmas came, I spent the holidays in Chicago. My folks had given me the name of a cousin and her husband who lived at Wilmette, a north Chicago suburb, but I had neglected to contact her. I was alone at Christmas . . . it was awful! So . . . I picked up a total stranger from off the street. The man was hungry and we enjoyed a holiday dinner together.

A month or so later, I wrote to my cousin, Florence Ustic. She promptly answered and invited me to visit. Next time I got leave, I did just that. Florence was quite a gal. Her husband Ray, had served a hitch in the Navy during the War and we swapped stories. As time passed, we became good friends.

At school, I was doing well and liked it. After we completed our first three months, a division was made. I found that our school was not only for aviation mechanics but was also for general machinest mates (those who operate the engines aboard ship and become marine engineers). I, along with over half of the class was transferred into steam engineering! A

121

serious mistake had been made. I had not enlisted for this and I lost no time in trying to get the mistake corrected.

I went to the office of the Senior Lieutenant who had charge of our school and registered my complaint. He got my file and pointed out to me that I had enlisted with a rating. They intended to take advantage of my training as an oiler and water-tender. My efforts and persistance in trying to get this mistake corrected resulted in my getting yanked out of school and put to work in the galley.

I peeled spuds every day for a week. Each day I would go see the lieutenant to try and get him to change his mind. Finally, he told me that if I came back again, he would have me thrown in the brig! That did it . . . I would have to find some other way to solve this predicament!

The Ustic's had asked me to spend Easter with them. I had been looking forward to that holiday and applied for liberty. I was promptly turned down. Later that evening, after dark, I changed into my liberty clothes, climbed over the camp fence and took a train to Chicago. That night I stayed in a hotel.

The next day, I went out to my cousin's at Wilmette. Florence was a good cook and Walter's tales of his experiences were always interesting. I enjoyed myself and the time passed quickly. When the "72 hour liberty" would have come to an end, I took my leave. Never did I mention to them any of my troubles, or what I had in mind.

Then for one whole week, I spent the time seeing the sights of Chicago. I went to the stock-yards and took in all there was to be seen there and in the evenings, I'd go to White City in South Chicago. They had a skating pavillion, a dance hall and everything else you might find in a carnival city. It was a great place to have fun!

On the ninth day, I took the train back to Great Lakes. I walked in the front gate and the guards asked for my leave papers. When I told them I had gone over the fence, they gave me an escort to the brig!

Two days later, along with twenty or more prisoners who were being held on a variety of charges, I was taken to court. Captain Wortsbaugh, commander at Great Lakes was holding court-marshals that day. I watched and listened as each, in his turn, was charged, pleaded and received various sentences.

When it was my turn, the charge against me was read: "Taking liberty without leave and being gone for nine days." After checking my record, the Captain said, "Young man, you have a good record . . . why did you do such a thing?" This gave me the chance I had been waiting for.

I told him why and he turned to one of his assistants with the order to "Check that out." Meantime, I was returned to the brig.

Several hours later, a release order came for me. I was to return to my school company . . . but, I was still in steam engineering.

When I started back to school, I decided I might as well go by the old saying, "If you can't beat 'em, join 'em." Thereafter, I did what was necessary to become a "General Machinist Mate."

Besides the school work, our company had been doing a lot of soldiering. We became good enough to win the privilege of representing the Great Lakes Naval Station at the "Pageant of Progress." Chicago was having a week-long celebration to record the completion of their new municipal pier. We were all excited as our company was transported by a sleek, small, navy ship to Chicago. There, next to the new municipal pier, on exposition grounds, our tent camp was set up.

We did our first bit of marching in the

opening parade. General Foch, the French War hero, acted as Grand Marshal. After that, we were allowed to enjoy everything that took place. There was a stunt flying and a parachute contest . . . carnival and all kinds of entertainment . . . a week fo fun! It was a great experience and I enjoyed every minute of it.

Several weeks after that, I received a letter from cousin Florence. She said my uncle John, Dad's oldest brother, with two of his daughters were going to be visiting the following weekend and could I come too?

When the time came, I was there. I met my uncle and two of the prettiest girls I ever did see. They were on their way home to Cincinatti, Ohio. They had been visiting my folks and other relatives on the west coast.

The girls, about 18 or 19 years old, had been considering becoming nuns. Their Dad, a railroad superintendant, had taken them on this trip before they made their final decision. I found it difficult to understand why two such lovely and talented girls would want to become nuns . . . they were a lot of fun.

Milwaukee, Wisconsin, is located about sixty miles north of Great Lakes. It was a place many sailors would go to spend their weekends. On its way north, the train, made a stop at Waukegan. People of that city didn't like people who smoke and had passed an ordinance prohibiting smoking. White lines had been painted marking the borders between railroad and city property. Smoking on the trains and within the railroad property was permissable. Just for fun, sailors and others who smoked, would chuck their cigarette butts over the line and into city territory. Waukegan's authorities didn't like this and many times things happened there. That's just what a lot of those young bucks were hoping for. Sometimes, it would become very exciting!

Finally, after nine months of schooling, we finished our training. I felt that I had passed my examinations okay . . . I was surprised when my name was called out at the graduation exercise I had passed third highest in a class of thirty eight and I received a bronze honor medal! Now I was a Machinist Mate 2nd Class . . . proud of my medal and my rating!

Within a few days, I was transferred to the Philadelphia Navy Base. Soon thereafter, I was assigned to a naval transport, the S.S. Chaumont. There, I was detailed to assist the Chief Petty Officer who had charge of maintenance of all mechanical equipment outside the fire and engine rooms. Besides other up-keep work, he gave me the job of taking care of the five galleys they had aboard. I would get up early in the mornings to help the cooks get their fires started. Lighting off those oil burning stoves gave the cooks troubles. If you didn't do it right, there would be a flare-back. That really scared some of those fellows. Odd thing . . . the Captain's private cook seemed to have more trouble than any of the others. That trouble continued until after I was invited to eat regularly with the help at the Captain's mess. Besides, there was an extra good spot near the galley for leisure time. I was encouraged to spend my spare time there . . . just in case the cook might need me.

Before leaving the East Cost, the ship took on a battalion of Marines bound for Nicaragua. I think the hardest thing for those Marines to learn aboard the ship was eating their meals standing up. Aboard the transport, space was scarce. Dining room for the troops were arranged with elevated, narrow, shelf-like tables. One had to stand while eating. If the going was not smooth, the place could become a mess.

Our ship took us down the east coast, crossed the Carribean, then through the

Panama Canal and northwesterly up along the Pacific side of Panama, Costa Rica and Nicaragua. The weather was ideal and we had a pleasant cruise. Each evening after dark, movies were shown. The moonlight nights in the warm southern waters left me with pleasant memories that I will never forget.

At Corinto, on the northwest coast of Nicauraga, we dropped anchor and our marines disembarked. They were all excited about possible action in that disturbed country.

Continuing on, our ship soon passed San Salvador, Guatemala and Mexico. As we approached the tip of Baja California, near the mouth of the gulf, we came onto a floatilla of turtles. There must have been thousands of them! Each one appeared to be the size of a large wash tub. How our ship kept from running them down, I'll never know.

At the entrance to the harbor at San Diego, the channel was narrow. That port was small, yet large enough to make a home for a good many naval ships.

We expected to be in port for several days and were glad when our turn came to go on liberty. San Diego was not a very large city, but it was an interesting one. I enjoyed beautiful Balboa Park very much. There were so many interesting things to see there.

Aboard ship one day, I got an unexpected surprise. Along with six other mechanics, I was transferred to the S. S. Vestal, repair ship for the Pacific Fleet. The Vestal was short of mechanics and the Chaumont had a surplus. Later that day, just after I finished packing, my name was called. I was ordered to report to the Executive Officer. He informed me that I was to be in charge of the transfer group. A package of records was handed to me with orders to deliver them to the Executive Officer of the Vestal when we arrived.

The Vestal too, was anchored in San Diego

Harbor. All of a sudden, while waiting for transportation, I got an idea. "Why not take a look at my record?" I quickly found myself a location with privacy. Opening my record, I took a good look . . . it was clean! Not one word of my "Nine Day Holiday," or my court marshal! HOORAY! No one ever found out, while I was in the Navy, that I had "checked" my record.

After arriving aboard the Vestal and delivering the package of records to the Executive Officer, I was assigned to the machine shop. There, I was shown a large lathe. I worked on the lathe in the daytime and slept over it at night. My hammock was stretched between its headstock and tailstock over the ways.

The Vestal was a very old ship and had been the repair ship for the Pacific fleet for a long time. All available space had been used for shops. Hardly any areas were left for human comforts. It was just a big floating factory with everything from foundries to the most delicate instrument repair shops. Aboard, they could manufacture or repair most anything.

Well do I remember my first job! I was handed a blueprint of a tap with the order "make that." That was a job for a tool maker but I drew the material and gave it a try. I bollixed the job. Needless to say, I found myself on that shop foreman's "shitlist!" I guess you know who got all the dirty work for some time to come.

Our home port was San Pedro (Los Angeles Harbor). During the winter months, the Vestal would anchor just inside the breakwater. It was quite a ways out in the harbor and it took nearly an hour to travel to the harbor dock. I attended night classes at San Pedro High School during this period. It was good to keep busy and the time passed much faster when I had things to do.

When summer came, our ship would make a run up the coast as far north as Bremerton in the Puget Sound. This way, each summer, most of the larger cities would be visited. It was a good way to learn the coast.

Each time we arrived in the Puget Sound, I would apply for a furlough. A couple of weeks spent visiting my folks in Portland was just great and I enjoyed every minute of it.

One time, on my returning to the ship after a furlough, I found everybody in the machinist's and electrical divisions restricted from liberty. There had been a fire in our division. Investigating officers couldn't find the cause and nobody was talking. Likewise, nobody was going ashore. That deadlock lasted until the ship left the Puget Sound area.

I was told that the fire had started in the electric shop. Some dumb guy was trying to solder up a leak in the small still he was operating. He started soldering without emptying the still and there was an explosion . . . followed by a fire. It started in some excelsior which was used in packing away breakable electrical equipment. There was a lot of smoke but little damage was done before it was put out and no one was hurt. However, it did cause a lot of excitement and sure put a crimp on the "liberty parties." Until we left Puget Sound, I was the only gob in that division going ashore.

One weekend, I took a trip to Everett, Washington to visit my uncle Jim. He was my father's youngest brother and was delighted to see me. He was a sawyer in one of Everett's largest lumber mills and went "all out" showing me everything around Everett and treating me like royalty. I enjoyed that weekend very much.

One day, I read a Notice on the ship's bulletin board:

WANTED
ANYONE WITH EXPERIENCE AS A PRINTER
REPORT TO THE EXECUTIVE

When I was a student at Jefferson High School, I had taken an extra subject, Printing. I went to the print shop and sized up the quarters. It was a palace compared to what I had. In addition, the printer looked like a pretty decent guy, so I went in and told him about my experience. He didn't say a word, but handed me a "printer's stick" (a small vice-like tool printers use to hold type they are setting) and pointed to a paragraph in the newspaper that was lying on the desk. I "set up" that paragraph and the printer took a proof. I had made several mistakes but that wasn't bad (considering the length of the paragraph).

Then he asked me, "How long since you studied printing in school?"

"Five or six years," I replied.

"Well, check that type box over a bit . . . you've forgotten where some of the letters are located."

I did as he suggested, then, after a while, he said, "Better go see the Executive. But don't tell him you've been in here."

I followed his instructions.

The Executive Officer brought me back to the print shop and instructed the printer to see if I knew anything about printing.

Again, I was handed a printer's stick. Pointing to the same paragraph in the newspaper that I had set up before, the printer said, "Set that up."

I did as I was told. This time, when the proof was taken, there was only one msitake! The Executive checked the proof and remarked, "Looks like we've found our man." That day, I was transferred to the print shop.

After several days work on my new job, I began to wonder why the printer needed extra help. The work we had to do was a breeze and I did most of it. My easy-going boss urged me not to get excited. He was expecting certain regulation books to be ordered and just wanted help . . . to assure him of his usual life style.

He was quite a character and really did have some life style. We soon became good friends. One deal he had going showed what he was capable of. He had convinced those in control of supplies that 'pure grain alcohol' was the only cleaner that would keep the presses clean and operating. He drew a gallon every other month and that kept him going . . . just about. . .

Another deal that he cut me in on was his stationery business. Box stationery would be purchased from Zellerback Paper Company by the case. It cost 18¢ a box and would sell for 40¢. With initials printed on the envelopes, the price was 75¢ to 90¢. Printed in gold, $1.25 . . . and with a small print of a ship $1.50. I did all the work and the split was fifty-fifty. There were over 400 men in the crew of the Vestal. In addition to that, there were crews of other ships that would be tied up alongside for repairs. Sailors do a lot of writing so our market was a good one.

When the ship was in San Pedro over weekends, I would get leave as often as possible and go visit my brother, Hugh, who was working and living in Los Angeles. We traveled all over the area and saw the sights together. It was a break for the both of us.

The second summer, when our ship made its trip north, it went into drydock at Bremerton. A clean-up painting and general overhaul job was due. Again, I was able to get a furlough and went home to Portland. Visiting my family was the main thing I did. Harold Gorman was one of my old buddies. He had gone through Benson Trade School and had become a pattern-maker. While visiting with him, he told me of an opportunity he had had, but couldn't handle . . . he lacked financing. I asked for more details. It seemed that Harold worked for the Reed's Patternworks, one of the best in Portland. They turned out excellent work, but Mr. Reed wasn't easy to do business with. One machine shop manager, Bill McVey, kept Harold busy full time just doing the work for that machine shop. The manager would come into Reed's shop, bring the blueprints directly to Harold, and in this way, avoid contact with Mr. Reed. Harold did the work and everybody was satisfied.

Bill McVey tried to get Harold to set up his own shop. He promised Harold all his business and said he would even help him get more. Harold was flattered but didn't have the money to get started.

This happened just a short time before I arrived. I asked Harold how much it would take to start a pattern shop. His answer was $1,000 . . . if care was used. Then I asked what kind of a deal he would make me if I was to put up the money. His answer . . . one half interest.

Soon thereafter, I stopped by the Reed Pattern Works to size it up and, after Harold finished work, we went to see Bill McVey. Bill did manage a good sized shop. He confirmed what Harold had told me and said there was a vacant place nearby that would be ideal for a pattern shop. Harold and I looked at the location. Harold was pleased with it and that same day, we formed a partnership.

That shop was rented and we went to work. The area was searched for second-hand machinery and we were able to purchase all we needed to make a start. Then we set it up and by the time my furlough was over, our shop was ready to do business.

My folks were pleased with what I had done. Just a few days before, my Dad and I had a good long talk. He tried to convince me that Oregon was the best place in the world to live and that I had been a rolling stone long enough. He told me what I already knew . . . that all the family wanted me to come home and stay.

After I returned to the ship, one of the first things I did was to go to the patternshop and talk to the patternmaker in charge. I told him I was interested in learning the trade.

He said, "We just got an order to change over certain patterns from wood to metal. We could use a machinist mate". I got the job and was transferred pronto! . . . I felt "right bad" about losing my income from the stationary business. In the long run, however, I would be better off.

Patternmaking is a very important and interesting trade. Usually an apprenticeship runs five years. Patterns are made from wood and are necessary for the construction of most every machine. Sometimes when mass production is intended, they are made of metal. In foundries patterns are needed for every type of metal casting. It was an interesting challenge for me and I tackled the work with enthusiasm . . . When the ship returned to San Pedro, I went ashore each evening and attended night school.

One day, about a week before Christmas, I received a telegram from home. My father was seriously ill! Obtaining a special leave, I contacted my brother Hugh and we made the trip home to Portland via Southern Pacific.

Our train arrived early the morning of the 22nd . . . but it wasn't early enough. Dad had passed away a few hours before! What a terrible shock! Grief over a loved one is always hard . . . and when it happens just before Christmas, it's just that much worse. I was thankful I was able to stay for several days following the funeral . . . Mother needed help. To make it easier for her, Hugh decided to stay home and I returned to San Pedro alone.

Back aboard ship, I worked hard to put our recent loss out of mind. One day, I was doing some delicate work, using a very old band saw. The upper and lower 36" wheels which carried the saw blade were made of heavy cast iron and the saw jumped its tracks. I switched off the motor and carefully held the piece with which I had been working, while the saw slowed down. My eyes were on the work so I didn't notice the upper wheel as it gradually made its way off the shaft. That wheel dropped to the steel deck, spinning at a rapid rate. It bounced, striking me on my left thigh and knocking me into a bulkhead some distance away! Fortunately, the machine stopped before anyone else was hurt. For many years, I suffered pain in my hip and back.

Paul Nester and the gun he was assigned to on the S.S. Vestal.

CHAPTER 8

BUSINESS IN PORTLAND

1923 - 1924

Shortly after I arrived in San Pedro the first time, Hugh and I purchased a lot in Los Angeles. Just before I got my discharge from the Navy, an attempt was made to sell that lot . . . it wasn't easy. Finally, a trade was made for our equity . . . we were now owners of a very nice new Chandler touring car.

By advertising in one of the Los Angeles papers, I was able to get four passengers who wanted to travel north. This would help me pay for my trip home to Portland. Early one saturday morning, we pulled out. The trip over the ridge on that narrow road between Los Angeles and Bakersfield (in those days) was quite an experience. Usually it took four or five hours to traverse those hundreds of mountainous turns as we climbed to an altitude of well over 4000 feet. Everything went alright until we were on that twenty mile straight-away just before you get to Bakersfield.

There, our car burned out a bearing. Quickly gathering some old rusty barb-wire from alongside the road for a tow-line, we flagged down a passing motorist and got a tow into Bakersfield. Saturday afternoon, the Chandler Agency was just closing. We made a deal to use their outside pit and the parts man promised to come back and sell us parts when he found out what was needed.

Thank goodness one of my passengers was an auto mechanic. He and I went to work. We tore the motor apart and found a burned out con-rod bearing. The parts man, as he had promised, came down and in short order we had a new one installed.

Soon, we were underway. My new friend, the mechanic, offered to spell me on the driving. This turned out to be a good break for me. He also helped me improve my driving ability. When we arrived at his home in Dunsmuir, Northern California, I was sorry to lose him.

Sometime after we passed the Oregon State line, we were making our way through beautiful mountains, freshly covered with snow. As evening approached, our motor started missing. We were able to make it into a tiny village in a picturesque mountain valley. There, we stopped at a combination blacksmith shop/garage. The mechanic told us we were in Myrtle Creek. He refused to look at our motor until after he had his supper. However, he did take time to tell us how good the food was at the Inn's boarding house. We were all hungry so we ate there. A bunk in the bunkhouse only cost 25¢. After a fine breakfast the next morning, the mechanic found the trouble with our motor. It was in the magneto. He had that motor purring like a kitten in a jiffy. Soon we were on our way north again. Many times in the years since, when passing near Myrtle Creek, memories of those fabulous meals and that overnight stay in that beautiful valley would come back to me.

The next day, we arrived in Portland. My welcome home was, as always, a happy one.

136

This time however, I intended to stay. After a short initial visit, I got around to asking about Harold and how the shop was doing. My mother assured me Harold was fine and that I would be surprised when I visited the shop.

Sure enough, I was surprised. When I walked into the shop, besides Harold, there were four other patternmakers at work. I found out Harold had been quite successful in getting all the work he and his small crew could handle. He was good at estimating contracts and was well liked by those with whom he did business. Gorman and Nester Patternworks was doing well and we both were pleased and proud!

Within a few days, I started to work. It was a new experience for me . . . working as a partner in my own business. Our shop hours were from eight to five o'clock mondays through fridays. Saturdays we worked till noon. Most of the men, in order to have saturdays off, would work overtime other days of the week. Harold and I would alternate so we could have every other saturday off.

One day, shortly after arriving home, I met Katherine Danaher. We had not seen each other since Johnnie (our nephew) was baptized. The two of us had been John's Godparents. Katherine had become quite an attractive girl! We started going out together and soon became very good friends. That spring (and from then on), we enjoyed being together, seeing all the interesting things there are to be seen and enjoyed by the young people around Portland.

That fall, both Harold and I wanted to go hunting. Since one of us had to stay home and keep shop, we couldn't go together. So we tossed a coin to see who would be lucky and I won. Early one morning, Hugh and I with Harold's younger brother Marvin, took off and headed for the high Cascade mountains south of Mt. Hood. We stopped at the ranger station near Government Camp. There we were advised not to get too far back in those mountains as it was late in the season and a snow might catch us.

After driving south for an hour or so, we parked. Shouldering our packs, we headed west. We followed a ridge out of the timber and headed up to a remote lake. Each time we came to the division of a ridge, I would remind my hunting partners to pay particular attention to our route. That country would look entirely different when covered with snow.

Carrying supplies, in addition to our bedding and rifles, we were pretty well loaded. I was in the lead, Marvin followed and Hugh brought up the rear. Suddenly there was the blast of a shot being fired! I felt the hot air as a bullet passed close to my right hand and arm! Marvin's rifle had accidentally discharged! He had been hiking along with the hammer cocked and with his finger on the trigger. I was very lucky that day and from then on, Marvin walked in front!

Late that afternoon, after a sixteen mile hike, we arrived at the lake. We made camp, gathered wood and drew straws to see who would cook our first meal. Marvin was it. Hugh and I tried our hand at fishing and then gathered a good supply of huckleberries.

We hadn't realized Marvin knew nothing about cooking and he was having his troubles. Intending to cook a pot of beans, he filled the pot half full of beans, then filled it up with water! He now had most all the containers full of swelling and overflowing beans! For supper that night, I mixed up some batter and we had huckleberry pancakes.

About the time it started to get dark, it began to rain. We rigged up a tarp lean-to and by that time the rain had turned to snow. Our supply of firewood was good so we rolled up in our blankets and were soon sound asleep.

Suddenly, I was aroused. Hugh was up and was wrestling around with his blanket, trying to put out a fire! After a fair sized hole was burned in his blanket, he succeeded. It seems that Hugh had awakened earlier, cold. The fire was down so he moved it over a bit and built it up good . . . too good. Then he took the warm ground for his bed. He was soon asleep but when he awoke, his blanket was on fire. All the excitement and exercise of putting the fire out warmed him up! He slept well for the rest of the night.

Next morning there was six inches of snow on the ground! We made our breakfast and discussed our predicament. We decided to get out of there before the snow got any deeper. Packing, Marvin said he wasn't going to haul out any of the food supplies he had packed in. Hugh and I objected and there was an argument. We told Marvin it might take us a week to make our way out . . . that if he didn't pack his share, he wouldn't get one bite of ours. Finally, he gave in and agreed to pack his share.

We took turns breaking trail through the snow. About noon, we came to a division of the ridge. Marvin wanted to take a route that Hugh and I believed to be the wrong one . . . another argument. Finally, Hugh and I, tired of talking, started on our way . . . Marvin could do as he pleased! We hadn't gone far when here he came, following along. It's a good thing he did 'cause he never would have made his way out if he had gone the other way. We reached the car and left before the storm started again, dropping considerably more snow. I have been careful about who I go on a hunting trip with ever since.

At the shop, some things were bothering me more than Harold realized. We never had a bit of trouble with our crew. They understood the situation and helped me as much as possible. On saturdays, however, when I was there at the shop alone, if somebody walked in with a complicated blueprint and wanted me to figure a job, it put me on the spot. I couldn't tell them that I was only an apprentice, so I would try and get them to leave the prints. Usually though, they had some reason for not wanting to do this. Also, on most any work day, Harold would get a call and have to go to some machine shop or foundry to make an estimate on a job and I wouldn't see him for the rest of the day. Harold was doing a great job and I didn't mind his taking all the time he wanted . . . except when he was away. It left me right in the middle of a most embarrassing position. Harold was young, good looking and popular and I couldn't blame him. Little by little, though, his absence got to bugging me more and more. We talked about this. Harold just put it off as though it didn't mean a thing. We were each making more money than just about any skilled working man and I should have been satisfied.

I discussed my problem with Bill McVey and he came up with a possible solution. Our business had grown rapidly. Why not incorporate? With a three man corporation, Harold might be more easily encouraged to get back on the job . . . at least we hoped he would. We did incorporate. Harold and I each got 45% of the stock, Bill paid cash for the remainder. The change helped . . . for awhile . . . then the situation worsened.

About that time, my attention was attracted to the work of a foundryman who had been getting patterns made at our shop. John Carry had developed a system of pouring concrete castings. With the proper patterns and moulding sands, he could make almost anything. He was planning to start his "Cast Stone" business soon and felt Southern California was the place to situate . . . that country was developing fast.

I made a deal with Carry, sold out my patternshop interest to Bill McVey and prepared to leave for Southern California.

When they heard what I had done, Katherine and my entire family were shocked. They tried hard to get me to change my mind, but it was too late. I had already made my move.

Katherine Danaher.

Paul Nester.

CHAPTER 9

LOS ANGELES

1924 - 1925

Carry and I were packed and on our way south within a week. Our trip to Los Angeles was uneventful. After finding a satisfactory place to room and board, we spent maybe a week touring Los Angeles, looking things over and searching for a suitable place to start our operation. We did find, in southeast Los Angeles, a building with adequate fenced yard space. We rented it for a reasonable fee and on the building we painted our sign "Cast Stone Products Company." While I was getting things properly set up inside the building, Carry searched for the proper moulding sands and scouted for business.

Getting started wasn't as easy as we thought it would be. I commenced to wonder whether I had done the right thing . . . selling the interest in my patternmaking business and leaving Portland in such a hurry. For the first time in my life, I began to get homesick. I missed Katherine and every one of my family.

John Carry and Paul Nester with their telephone
conduits.

Then one day, Hugh showed up. He had got itchy feet to come back to Southern California. You know . . . I was able to talk Hugh into returning to Portland with me. We were preparing to leave when we received word from Mother that she had sold our home in Portland and was heading south. The family wanted to be with Hugh and I in Los Angeles so, that put an end to dreaming about returning home to Portland.

Soon, after that we got our first order. Water meter boxes for a large subdivision. I made the patterns and we got busy . . . our plant was finally in operation.

While traveling about Los Angeles, Carry and I had noticed quite a few street construction jobs underway. Clay conduits were being installed underground for the telephone company. When properly installed, they formed the passageway for telephone cables. Carry examined some of those conduits and concluded that with the proper patterns we could make them in concrete. I went to work on this and soon we were producing two, four and six way concrete telephone conduits.

Carry then contacted Mr. E.A. Imer, the largest local contractor in the installation field. He made a visit to our plant. When he saw what we could do, he immediately wanted an interest in our company. Mr. Imer put up the funds for expansion, we incorporated and now, we were assured of a good continuous market.

Within a reasonable time, we were going full blast with a fair sized crew. Even Hugh went to work for us. Telephone conduits and water meter boxes were our main products.

Mother purchased a duplex on 56th Street just west of Broadway and Hugh and I were living at home. It was wonderful to be back with the family again. Our home was located not too far from where we worked.

One weekend when I was cruising around

in my new Ford roadster south on Western Avenue, I passed the Burdette Fuller Airport. My eye caught sight of a large sign advertising their flying school. Curious, I went in and inquired.

Mr. Fuller wanted to know why I wanted to learn to fly. I told him of my old time dream of "Learning to fly so that I could become a 'Bush Pilot' in Alaska." He mentioned stunts . . . would I be able to take them? I couldn't see where that was necessary but answered if it was, I would learn about them too. Next thing I knew, Fuller and I were up in a "Jennie."

It was a marvelous feeling and I was thoroughly enjoying it! We climbed to perhaps 1500 feet when the plane went into a tail-spin. After several revolutions, Fuller brought it out of the spin and came in for a landing.

Back at the office, he explained to me, "The Curtis Wright JND4's, (Jennies) are military surplus training planes left over from World War I. They were built to train pilots. Structurally they are the greatest, but they only have OXX5, 90 horsepower engines. They are under-powered and cannot climb steeper than 6°. Any steeper and the plane stalls and goes into a spin. That's why it is necessary to learn stunts in order to become a good pilot."

Twice a week, in the evenings, I would drive to the airport and take my lessons. Very soon, I found out that Burdette Fuller had been a fighter pilot and a Captain in the Air Force during the War. His school had the reputation of turning out the best pilots one could find in the Los Angeles area. He employed several young aviators who did most of the flight instruction. My instructor was usually Jack Frys, a young chiropractor about my age who loved to fly. We got along well and I learned a great deal from him. One day after I had been taking lessons for six weeks or two months, when I went to the airport, Jack was not there.

Fuller sent me out with another flier, Hap Rodell. To start, our flight was the usual climb to 1500 feet or so. That was a good maneuvering altitude. Hap signalled for me to take over then he climbed out of the cockpit, hung his legs over the forward edge of the lower wing and started to slide out away from the fuselage!!! I thought he had gone crazy but I was so busy trying to keep that plane flying level that I didn't have time to worry about what went wrong with Hap.

Then I saw what he was doing. Half way out on the wings of that biplane was a set of struts. Hap put his arm around the forward strut and started tightening up a cable turnbuckle which had been unwinding. This was causing brace wires to go out of adjustment. Hap rewound the turnbuckle, tightening those wires, and made it fast with some dangling safety wire. After he finished that job, he slid back along the wing to the fuselage and climbed back into his cockpit. Finally, he signalled me to take her down. I brought the plane in for a perfectly smooth landing.

Hap told me to "stay put" and got out to examine the repaired turnbuckle. Satisfied, he came back around and hollered to me, "Take her off!" I yelled back, "I haven't soloed yet." He answered, "You'll never be any more ready than you are right now . . . take off!"

I did as ordered, but I think while making that low, wide circle around to the approach position, physically and mentally, I was tensed up more than I had ever been in my life. Then, all of a sudden I got a half sick feeling in my stomach . . . I was concerned about the condition of that plane as well as my ability to bring it in like I had so many times before . . . but always with an instructor. Thank goodness, I made that landing smooth as glass!

Burdette Fuller and Hap Rodell were standing outside the office building watching, so I taxied around to the starting area. They signalled me to take off again! This I did and this time I went around without experiencing that nauseating feeling in my stomach. However, when I made my landing, I did some bouncing. Those two were there again, signaling for me to go around once more! I made it a third time and bounced even more!

When I went into the office, I was congratulated by everybody and told I would need nothing more than solo experience . . . HOORAY! I could fly and do most any stunt any pilot wanted to do! I was a graduate of the best flying school in Southern California and I was proud! Thereafter, Burdette Fuller rented me a plane whenever I wanted to fly.

Early one saturday morning, I was out flying solo. I had followed the coast west of Santa Monica. A heavy fog rapidly came in off the ocean. I turned and followed the coastline back to Santa Monica. Flying low under the fog, I turned and flew just above Santa Monica Boulevard all the way to Western Avenue. There, I turned south and took Western all the way to the airport. Don't believe I was ever over 150 feet or so off the ground while following those two boulevards. After that experience, I knew the real meaning of the old flier's phrase, "Flying by the seat of your pants." After that, I paid much more attention to weather reports.

Once, when I called in to arrange for a plane, Fuller said, "Let's fly over to the Douglas Airport at Santa Monica. The 'Around the World' flyers are coming in and that should be well worth seeing."

Fuller and I flew over to Douglas Airport and got to see the two Douglas planes that made it "Around the World" come in! Four U.S. Army Douglas biplanes, powered with 400 horsepower Liberty engines, took off from Santa Monica April 6, 1924. One plane crashed in

Alaska in a bad fog. It's crew of two were not seriously injured but it took ten days for them to make it back to civilization. The second plane had engine trouble and had to come down on a jungle river in Indonesia. There they waited until another motor was shipped to them. After installation, they resumed their journey. The third plane was lost at sea somewhere between Iceland and Greenland. The crew however, was picked up by a small fishing trawler without injury. We witnessed the two planes that made it all the way, when they arrived at Douglas Field! First time ever, "Around the World!" . . . No one was seriously injured and they didn't lose a man!

One day, I had the opportunity of buying a Jeannie Canuck (a Canadian trainer) that had a Curtis Wright OXX6, 100 horsepower engine. This plane had ten more horsepower than the OXX5's used by the U.S. Army. It was in excellent condition and I was very proud of it.

When I was out flying my "Canuck" one sunday, I made a landing on a field alongside a well-traveled road south and east of Los Angeles. Motorists usually stop when they have an opportunity to see a plane parked nearby. One fellow hollered to me, "Give you five bucks for a plane ride." Right there, he got his nice long ride and I got into a brand new weekend business . . . BARNSTORMING! Even at $1.00 a ride, I could do all right.

From that time on, in the evenings, I would scout for satisfactory locations where I could fly passengers on weekends. I even put up signs at the locations letting people know about the rides on saturdays and sundays. Each time I arrived at the field, (wherever it was) I would come in at about 1500 feet, drop into a tailspin and make four or five revolutions before coming in for a landing. That was good advertising. Usually, I kept quite busy . . . three weeks at any one location was long

Opening day at Bell Airport.

Jennies take off to gain altitude for the "Dead Stick Landing Contest."

enough. Life was truly exciting!

In the spring of 1925, an aviator friend of mine told me about a field near the city of Bell. Bell's Chamber of Commerce was trying to promote the field for an airport. It wasn't far south and east of Los Angeles, so we went out to look it over. Located on the east side of Atlantic Boulevard, a short distance north of Florence Avenue, it appeared to be an ideal location.

Meeting with the officers of the Chamber of Commerce and the owner of the property, we made a deal. My friend and I formed a partnership and we each wound up a half owner of Bell Airport. Hangars and an office building were erected. When everything was ready, we held a Grand Opening. There was stunt flying, races, and a dead-stick landing contest. (Planes from all over the southwest showed up for that event). Thousands of people enjoyed the celebrations held there that sunday. It was a great success!

Thereafter, we operated our own Aviation School . . . that was my partner's job. For him, flying was a full time business. I still had my interest in the Cast Stone Porducts Company and worked weekdays from seven in the morning till four in the afternoon. Usually I would show up at the airport about five or five thirty in the afternoon and fly short hops until dark. Saturdays and sundays, I put in full time at the airport. Needless to say, we got off to a good start.

One day, an insurance salesman stopped by and talked to my partner and I. He told us that the New York Life Insurance Company was starting a program to see if it would be possible to insure aviators. For the first time ever, fifty aviators would be insured. Were we interested?

I was and my application was taken. Several days later I went into Los Angeles to

151

The two Jennies on the left were Bell Airport planes.

the doctor for my medical examination. After checking me over, the doctor said, "Sorry I have to turn you down! You have a bad heart! . . . By the way, do you smoke?"

"Yes, several cigars a day . . . good ones!"

"Well, I think that might be it. I'll bet you have what we call a 'Tobacco Heart.'"

I had noticed an odd feeling, especially after smoking, so I asked the doctor, "What if I quit smoking for a while then come back and see if I can pass your examination?"

The doctor thought that was a good idea. Six weeks passed and I sure missed my cigars. I returned to the doctor's office and the doctor made his examination. Completing that, he said, "You're fit as a fiddle. No trouble as long as you lay off the smoking." I got my insurance and I haven't smoked since.

At the Cast Stone Products Company, we were busy. Besides his usual jobs, (close around Los Angeles) Mr. Imer had landed a large contract to install conduits underground for the Telephone Company at Redlands. Our conduits would be used. We went to considerable expense, purchased all the materials, enlarged our crew, and worked for months turning out that order. When we started delivering the conduits to Redlands, the telephone company there refused to accept them.

There was a clause in the small print of that contract which gave the telephone company the right to refuse to accept any conduit which contained any trace of alkali. I don't believe any concrete product can be made in Southern California without a trace of alkali. Laboratory experts made tests of our product and reported that the slight amount of alkali in those conduits would do no harm to the lead sheathing of the cables (even after hundreds of years). That made no difference. It was plain

My partner's plane after the crash.

to us that that was the way the vitrified clay people had of eliminating the competition. After that, Mr. Imer was unable to get contracts with other telephone companies without that clause and THAT put us out of business!

Within a week after this setback, in the late afternoon, I arrived at the airport. As I stepped out of my car, I saw my partner's plane spinning TOO LOW! The plane spun into the ground and crashed! When I arrived at the scene, the passenger was dying and my partner was seriously injured . . . he was unconscious.

When he came to at the hospital, he explained to me that, this customer, a big heavy fellow, came in and said he wanted to learn to fly. He didn't know, however, about stunts. My partner suggested they "take a ride and see."

Roy made the fatal mistake of using his own plane which was equipped with dual controls instead of mine. When they got up to 1500 feet or so, Roy cut the throttle and the plane tipped over into a spin. After several revolutions, an attempt was made to bring it out. The rudder bar was over full to the right and, with all his strength, Roy's efforts couldn't budge it! The passenger in the front cockpit had slumped down very low in his seat. He had apparently passed out! Whether he had fainted or had a heart attack, or what, we don't know but his full weight was jammed against the rudder bar! The plane spun right into the ground and killed the man!

Serious injuries and deaths are always disasters. Losing two very good businesses, all in one week, wasn't very pleasant either. I did all I could . . . sold all I had to help pay for those hospital bills and for all the other expenses and damages.

I was broke and feeling pretty low. One day in December 1925, I went down to the railroad tracks east bound from Los Angeles

155

and hitched onto a freight train that was headed towards Florida.

At Tucson, Arizona, I found a job. The University of Arizona was building a new gymnasium at its school nearby. I was lucky, and went to work there helping in the construction. After my first pay day, I rented a room and started to eat regularly. Usually after work, I ate in a restaurant, then spent the evening at the library. That job lasted only about six weeks but it gave me time to do some thinking. I decided not to go further east but to go right back to Los Angeles.

One evening, after dark, when the west-bound passenger train stopped at Tucson, I climbed up on top the dining car (without being seen). I rode that train all the way to San Bernadino, California. Two nights later, I rode another passenger diner all the way to Los Angeles. Who says it can't be done? I do however, have some good advice: "Don't try it in the winter time. It's mighty cold up there."

Arriving in Los Angeles, I got myself a room in a cheap downtown hotel and then went looking for a job. I was sent from an employment office, along with several others to help unload freight cars at a warehouse. That job lasted only a couple days. When we were about finished the boss called me aside and asked if I would like to work there. I answered "yes" and he instructed me to return in the morning. I worked several months at that warehouse and when I finished I was driving a Mack truck. Evenings I spent in the library and I took every Civil Service examination that came up.

CHAPTER 10

LOS ANGELES COUNTY SHERIFF'S DEPARTMENT

1926

My first call to go to work was from the Los Angeles County Sheriff's Department. I didn't know a thing about police matters, but figured I could learn. Late in July of 1926, I was sworn in as a deputy sheriff and went to work in the newly constructed Hall of Justice. The Sheriff's Office took up the entire first floor of that building and also supervised the top four floors which housed the county jail. The county Assessor and Coroner also had offices in this building. The rest of it was used for Superior Courts.

Sheriff's are officers of the Superior Courts. They enforce the laws in unincorporated territories and investigate felonies in their assigned areas. My first assignment was the graveyard shift out of the main downtown office. A captain was in charge and he had two crews of three men each. Two deputies and the driver of a Cadillac made up each crew.

The first night I worked, business was slow . . . no calls for the first several hours.

About four o'clock in the morning, the Captain asked me if I'd like to take a walk. He took me down to the basement of that big new building. Next thing I knew, he was looking over the corpses! We were in the Coroner's office . . . the morgue! There were a lot of bodies lying on those cold slabs! The Captain told me that the day before in a bootleggers squabble two hijackers had been shot and he thought he might know one of them.

Several days after that, our crew was dispatched to the Constable's office at Norwalk. There, we picked up a man on an insane warrant. We were on our way to transport this fellow to the psychoward of the General Hospital. As we drove along Boyle Avenue in Belvedere Gardens, we stopped for a traffic signal. A man leisurely walked past in the crosswalk directly in front of our car . . . he was nude . . . not a stitch of clothes on him!

My partner said, "Did you see what I saw?" Our passenger, who was strapped up alongside of me in the back seat said, "Hey look! That guy's crazier than I am!"

When the signal turned green, Lindy, our driver, made a U-turn and came alongside our nuddie. My partner and I both got out of the car and stopped him . . . but only for a moment. He took off like an antelope! We both started after him and at first, I was gaining. My partner kept hollering, HALT . . . HALT . . . HALT . . . then he fired a shot in the air, thinking that might help . . . but it didn't! That guy ran faster than ever. I was able to keep him in sight and, after several blocks, he must have lost his wind. Now, I was gaining fast. He turned and ran up to the front door of a house where I got a half-nelson on him.

About that time my partners arrived with the car. The people of that house came out to see what the rumpus was all about. They didn't know our nuddie and wanted no part of him! In

158

due time, both our passengers were delivered to the psycho-ward of the hospital.

Later that morning before we went off shift, we got a report from the hospital. It seems our nuddie was just a sleep-walker out doing his thing.

I hadn't written home for several months . . . not even to Katherine. There was no way of telling what she might think about the accident or about the business failures I had experienced. I did know how she felt about my flying . . . she didn't like it! I wrote Katherine a good long letter. After mailing it, I went home and apologized to my mother and family for running out on them. They were all happy to see me and insisted that I stay there with them. This I was glad to do.

I worked on the graveyard shift for two weeks. Then, the regular deputy returned from his vacation and I was once again assigned to the bullpen. That was a holding area where deputies, working out of the main office, spent their time between calls. Lieutenant Calvert was the assignment officer on the day shift.

At that time, there were two sub-stations operating in county territory . . . Florence avenue and Belvedere Gardens. Each station took care of the business in its specific area. There was over 400 square miles to police. Just one investigation from the main office would sometimes take a full eight hours. Upon returning from any investigation, a full report had to be made to the Record Bureau.

A number of specialized details operated from the Sheriff's Office, such as Homicide, Robbery, Burglary, Auto Theft, Forgery, Cattle Theft and the Liquor and Vice Details. Deputies assigned to any one of those details became experts in their line. For new deputies, there was no such thing as a police school. New deputies were always assigned with the old-timers and learned from them. Regular

159

civilian clothes were the uniforms.

One day, three of us "green-horn" deputies were talking in the bullpen. Lieutenant Calvert approached and said, "I've got three jobs for you fellows. One in homicide, one in auto theft and one in the jail . . . who wants what?" The other two fellows spoke right up. They wanted the homicide and auto theft jobs. They were detailed. After they left, the Lieutenant asked me if I had any preference. My answer was "You're the boss. I'll go wherever you send me." He must have liked my answer for he said, "I'm going to send you to the jail . . . but it won't be for long. I think I'll send you to one of the new sub-stations that will be operating shortly."

I was assigned to the jail, to work the graveyard shift. I had the ninth floor all to myself. The kitchen, dining room, hospital, padded cells and quarters for the trustees were all located there. Every twenty minutes, I made a complete round . . . just like when I worked in the engine room aboard ship. I was told that the average stay in the jail was at least six months. Even though jail duty could become very monotonous, I accepted it.

Then one autumn day when I only had been working in the jail for about one month, I was ordered to the main office bullpen. Reporting there, I found a very large room packed with deputies. We didn't have to wait long when Harry Wright, the Chief Criminal Deputy and Lieutenant Calvert entered.

Harry Wright, a very tall and powerful appearing man, called out four men and introduced each as a Captain of one of the four new sub-stations then he directed each captain to a different corner of the large room. Ray Conley would be Captain of station #3, Temple; Johnny Neighbors, Captain of station #4, Vermont; Bill Horton, Captain of station #5, Norwalk; Jeb Stewart, Captain of station #6,

Newhall. Lieutenant Calvert then called the names of eight deputies and directed them to go to the corner and report to Captain Conley of station #3. That was done in turn for each remaining station. I was assigned to the group at Norwalk station.

Paul Nester at Newhall.

CHAPTER 11

NEWHALL

1926 - 1927

Then Harry Wright called for a volunteer. One of the men who lived with his family in Norwalk was assigned to Newhall. Could a swap be arranged? Quite a few of the fellows knew each other, but aside from Lieutenant Calvert, I didn't know a man there. All I knew about the lieutenant was just who he was. I took a fast look at the group in the Newhall corner and liked what I saw there. So I volunteered and was re-assigned to Newhall.

Newhall was a small village, located in a picturesque valley in the foothills of the Tehechapi Mountains. It was on the Ridge Route Highway, twenty one miles north of Los Angeles. All traffic on the inland route north, plus that going northeast through Lancaster and Mojave, passed that way. The Southern Pacific railroad tracks also went through Newhall. Our station was located in one of two small cottages on the main highway at the south edge of town. The Forestry Station occupied the other cottage.

Jeb Stewart, our captain, was a newlywed

and he and his wife had just moved to Newhall. He was a brand new captain, too. That first day, all the deputies met at the station. Our Captain gave us a short talk and then assigned partners and posted a work schedule. I would be working with Primus Kuneau. We would be on the four till twelve midnight shift. Roy Ernst and Bob Fox would work the graveyard shift while Jay Morley and Howden would work days. Shifts would be rearranged each month. Stockwell, Ed Adams and C.C. White would be relief men.

A couple of weeks after that, Kuneau was off and I was working the day shift with White. He was a tall slender fellow quite a bit older than I. We happened to be out on the front porch when we heard the clatter of hoofs on the pavement. Coming from the south, we saw what appeared to be a team of runaway horses, hauling a light delivery wagon, traveling downhill at break-neck speed . . . without a driver! They were headed for Newhall.

Both White and I ran to the roadway. My partner, with his long legs, made a running grab at the bridle of the nearest horse as it passed but missed. I made a run alongside the wagon, and as it passed, I grabbed the chain that held up the wagon gate! The gate was hanging open! Now I had my chance . . . first, to be dragged then to climb up into the wagon and over the seat. The reins were dragging and out of my reach. I was able to make my way down onto the tongue, then out between those horses and, finally, to straddle the horse on the right hand side. From there, I got ahold of the reins near the horse's mouth and brought the team to a halt!

By that time, we were right in front of the main general store, fairly close to the hotel and the blacksmith shop. You might say, right in the center of town. It looked like everybody was there! What I did was good advertising for our new station. Later, the owner of that runaway team came by the station to thank us. He said, "It's a lucky thing you mounted the horse you did, the other one never has been broke for riding and has always been a problem!"

The area around Newhall was ideal for the making of Western Moving Pictures. Because of this, Movie Companies would be on location there often. Usually they would stop by our office and let us know where they would be working. Many times, they would hire some of us off-duty deputies to work as extras. Roy Ernst and I were about the same age and we would always take advantage of this "extra" work. Roy was one quarter Indian and had served a hitch in the U.S. Calvary. He was an expert bare-back rider and got extra money for this. If I had a saddle, I made a pretty fair cowboy. Anyway, we both had a lot of fun and got good pay for it too.

Roy had another hobby . . . trapping. He put out and tended a line of traps in the nearby hills. Coyotes, fox and some of the smaller varmints were plentiful. We always could tell when Roy had had bad luck . . . trapping a skunk was usually <u>our</u> bad luck as well as <u>his</u>.

At the station, there was an extra room which was not being used. Kuneau and I got permission from the captain to bunk in it and to "batch" in the station kitchen. For that privilege, we would take care of any calls that might come in while the regular on duty crew was out on a call.

At times accidents, or some other emergency would occur up on the ridge. It took hours just to get to Gorman. Sometimes it would be in the Palmdale or Lancaster areas. On occasion, the on-duty crew would be called out and not be back until well into the next shift. Kuneau and I could take care of anything

165

reported to the station while the crew was out. We got in on all the excitement and enjoyed it.

One time, my partner and I were working the four till twelve shift when we got a call . . . a holdup in the Bakersfield area. They thought the culprits were headed our way. Going to Saugus, we set up a stake-out there at the intersection. Checking the passing cars, we found a suspicious one and had the driver park while we placed a telephone call to the record bureau. In those days, this was our only way of checking. Our stake-out was right in front of a restaurant and the driver of that car asked if he could go in and have a cup of coffee. He was given permission and we watched him enter the cafe. Other on-coming cars distracted us for a minute or so. When I looked back at the restaurant, the guy wasn't there. He had walked right through and out the back door into the dark!

About fifteen minutes later, we got word that the car he had been driving was hot. That fellow spent the entire night wandering around in the dark and by daylight, wound up in a canyon near Newhall.

At dawn, that morning, Roy started out to run his trap line. As he passed the station, one of the deputies on duty called to him, "Roy, if you see a fellow up there, wearing a sheepskin coat, bring him in. He got away from the four-to-twelve crew last night."

Sure enough, Roy hadn't gone far (heading up a dead-end canyon) when he met a man in a sheepskin coat.

"Good morning," Roy said. "Going to town?"

"Yes, I've been working on this ranch back up the canyon for some time. Need a bit of a vacation."

Roy knew there was no ranch back up that canyon and felt pretty sure he was the wanted fellow . . . but he didn't know for what and whether or not he was armed. Roy did have a little old .22 pistol he used for taking care of trapped animals and, with that, he marched the fellow back to the sheriff's station.

The Auto Theft Detail wanted this guy badly. It seems he had worked out a system of stealing cars in Oregon and Washington, transporting them to California and selling them there. His system had worked for several years. An end was put to that, however . . . at least for awhile.

That fall, when the deer hunting season opened up, Roy and I went hunting. I was working the day shift and had to be back by eight o'clock. I was on time with a beautiful buck, antlers still in the velvet. The fellows at the station accused me of having corralled that deer just waiting for the season to open.

I was having a lot of fun at Newhall, but realized I should get busy and do something which would put me in a better position for the future. There being no night school available within reasonable distance, I started a correspondence course in Law with the La Salle Extension University. I managed to study several hours most every day. Never had I planned to be a lawyer but thought the knowledge of law might help me later.

On occasion, two old-time deputies, Charlie Catlin and Bill Hanby, who made up (for the most part) the "Cattle Theft Detail" would stop by our station. A good part of their business was in our territory and, at times, they would get Roy and I to go along with them on a job. When that happened, we sometimes got a chance to do some riding. We always learned something when we were out with these men and we also enjoyed helping them.

One day the Captain told me he wanted me to work with Howden. He said several of the other deputies had trouble getting along with him. Howden was sort of a southern gentleman type and gave the impression that he was the "whole cheese." Also, they didn't like his attitude towards prisoners or even a person under investigation. The captain said, "If you can't work with him, he's had it."

The first shift Howden and I worked together, I told him exactly why I came to be his partner. If he was ever going to change his ways, he'd have to know this. That man, when he worked with me, was a perfect partner.

Then one day, I really got a shock. Howden was off and I was working the shift with Ed Adams. Ed was a tall, six foot four beanpole-type and about 40 years old. He was a Canadian war veteran . . . a rugged fellow and quite a man. Ed was sitting at the front desk and I was in the rear of the building. Howden came in the front door, drew his .38 Colt, levelled it at Adams and said, "I'm going to kill you, you dirty son-of-a-bitch, etc., etc., etc.!" As I walked into the front office, Howden swung the gun towards me and added, "Stay out of this, Paul. This is none of your business." I stopped cold as Howden, again, covered Adams. I never saw a man act and talk as deliberate and calm in all my life as Adams did when he told Howden, "All you have to do, Howden, is pull that trigger and my troubles will be over. But yours will just be starting. Think of all you're letting yourself in for. Don't know whether you like gas or just plain hanging, but if you pull that trigger . . . one or the other is what you'll get."

While Adams was talking, I saw Kuneau silently coming up the front steps. Apparently, he had heard some of the talk and had seen the startled look on my face. Kuneau got close in back of Howden then, at the nod of his head, we both jumped. Kuneau grabbed him from the rear and I got his gun arm. We disarmed and handcuffed him, then reported it to our captain. Howden was immediately transferred to the main office. Before the investigation was completed, however, he quit his job. Their trouble was over a woman! After resigning from the Sheriff's Department, Howden went to work for the LA Police Department. In a comparatively short time, he worked himself up to Captain rating. Eventually, he was shot throught the head in an action that was honorable and heroic. He died in the line of duty.

On occasion, I had gone out with Marion Firth, a pretty redhead who worked in Newhall and lived with her parents there. A group of young people had planned a beach party on the coast, west of Ventura. Monica, my 16 year old sister had been wanting to come to Newhall and see where her brother worked. When I told Marion, she invited Monica to come stay with her and go to the beach party with us. The day we went on the party, I introduced Monica to a young friend of mine, Al Shaw, who worked for the Mobile Oil Company at their plant in Newhall. Al took Monica to the beach party and he's been taking her everywhere else for the last 54 years!

The department held regular monthly shooting contests at the Sheriff's Range. Competition was strong between the teams of the various sub-stations and the downtown details. Roy Ernst, Ed Aitkens and I were all on the Newhall team. Out in our country, we got plenty of practice.

Along about this time, some of the Owens Valley Ranchers and others up in the valley, believing they had received a bad deal from the Los Angeles Water Department, threatened to blow up dams and the acqueduct system. Most of these facilities were located in our territory, so a lot of extra patroling was being done.

One day, Roy and I were working extra on this patrol. We were traveling slowly on a far out desert road alongside the aqueduct when we

COUNTY OF LOS ANGELES

SHERIFF

LOS ANGELES, CALIFORNIA

June 30, 1927

To All Sub-Stations:

Wish at this time to call your attention to the fact that squads from the Main Office are making some wonderful shooting scores. During the last season, the Sub-Station Division stood at the top of the list, and it is embarrassing to be the butt of their friendly ridicule along this line.

The Sub-Station Division has the material for good marksmen, and I am asking that in the future, when on the range, that more attention be given to making every shot count, than merely to getting through. When off the range, daily trigger squeeze and sighting practice, will be a great benefit. All will be surpirsed at its results.

I wish at this time, to compliment several of the men on the marked improvement in their shooting, particularly Mr. E. M. Burt, who has advanced shooting score from that of 60 a year ago, to the score of 199 at the last shoot. Mr. C. C. White, has advanced from about the same score, to an average of 176. This shows the result of practice and perseverance.

Congratulations are extended to Mr. Wm. White, of Sub-Station #5, for the score of 228, in the last shoot. Also to Mr. Paul Nestor, of Sub-Station #6, with score of 232, being the high score of the Division.

I would suggest that each station captain, appoint a man who is familiar with the rudiments of shooting, to take charge of the station team, in an endeavor to bring it to the top. If the captains will turn over to me, the names of team captains, I will issue necessary orders, and see that they are obeyed.

Several prizes are to be offered in the fall, for shooting. I want the sub-stations to be in on it, and win. I will do all possible to help any man, but with the great number of men and distance between stations, I cannot give every man individual attention.

I feel that all will respond, if they have the interests of the sub-station at heart, as we are making good in other respects, for which I wish to express my thanks.

Respectfully,

Col. W. M. Hotz,

Asst. Chief Deputy, Crim. Divn.

spotted a jack rabbit some distance away. I stopped the car and we both got out. In the winter, rabbit is good eating. Because of the distance, we decided to both shoot at the count of three. One . . . two . . . bang! Roy shouted, "I got him!" I thought maybe, "I got him too!" We paced the distance off and it was just over 50 yards! We both got him! One shot blew off his head and the other messed up his stomach . . . not bad for pistol shooting. Only thing . . . there wasn't much left worth eating.

Placerita Canyon lies east from Newhall. Its mouth opens into the Santa Clara Valley just across the railroad tracks. It is well named for it produced gold many years before what is generally supposed to be the first discovery of gold, at Sutter's Mill, California in 1848.

Roy had been wanting to learn how to recover placer gold and I wanted to see if there was enough left to make it worthwhile. We went to work and did recover some small nuggets. However, I figured we better not continue or we would have troubles. Most of that area was privately owned and the owners wouldn't like it if we messed up their property.

We started a search for likely mineral areas where the land was open and could be staked. In the Ventura County Recorder's Office we found records of an old mining district. The Castaic Mine was located in that district some miles to the southwest of Mt. Frazier.

Roy and I were delighted with the far-away primitive area. The remoteness appealed to us and there were some good, possible mining prospects. From then on, we spent a considerable amount of time in those mountains.

One day, I really got a surprise . . . a telephone call from Katherine. She was on vacation and had come from Portland to San

Pedro by boat . . . an ocean trip. She was staying at the Figueroa Hotel. We hadn't seen each other for a mighty long time, so I made arrangements for time off. Katherine and I both discovered that we missed each other more than we cared to admit. We spent the balance of her vacation time seeing the sights around Los Angeles and taking trips out to the Newhall country where I worked.

One winter afternoon, our regular crew had been out on a call for some time. The telephone rang. An assult and robbery had taken place up on the Ridge Route near Gorman. Kuneau was not available so I asked Roy, who happened by, if he would go with me. He agreed and we made the long run up to Gorman.

The victim told us this story: "He was a musician on his way north to San Francisco. Driving his Chevrolet sedan through San Fernando, he picked up two hitch-hikers. One rode up front with him and the other sat in the back. Traveling through the mountains, he was suddenly hit in the head with a blunt instrument and knocked out. When he regained consciousness, he was down in a deep ravine alongside the highway, in the snow and mud. He was able to make his way back up to the road and flag down a passing motorist who brought him into Gorman. The people there cleaned him up and dressed his wound, and then called the Sheriff's Office. He was fortunate, he was not seriously wounded but he was concerned about the loss of an accordian he had had in the rear seat of his car.

I got the phone and forwarded this information to the Sheriff's Office at Bakersfield. It was past seven o'clock by this time and I was hungry. Having hardly any money with me, I was about to ask Roy for a loan when he said "Paul, I left without my pocketbook. Could you loan me the price of a meal? I'm hungry!"

We both searched our pockets and between us, came up with 60¢. At least that was enough for donuts and coffee. When we were finished, we had 30¢ so we invested it in a slot machine. WOW! We won enough for each of us to go back and have a fine meal.

As we finished eating, a telephone call came in from the Bakersfield Sheriff's Office. They reported the capture of our culprits. I called our Main Office and got permission to go north and pick them up.

At the Bakersfield Sheriff's Office, they told us that Delano, like so many of the small towns of California, had just one officer on shift at a time. Also, like so many of the smaller places, the station made a good hang-out for friendly people. One old timer was there when our "Want Broadcast" came in. These things he remembered when he left the station that evening: "Look for a Chevrolet sedan with two men and an accordian case in the back seat." As he crossed the street, a Chevrolet with two men pulled up and parked at the cafe. When the men entered the cafe, our friend walked up and casually took a look into the back seat. There was the accordian case. He returned to the Sheriff's station and told the deputy. The two scoundrels were under arrest and in jail mighty fast.

Roy and I proceeded to Delano and picked up the felons. The victim's car and property had been safely stored for him and he was a very thankful man. It was past midnight when Roy and I got back to Newhall with our prisoners. I was plenty tired and a bit late for the start of my next twelve to eight a.m. shift. Luckily, we didn't have any calls and I slept right on through the shift.

One morning, I was working the early shift with Stockwell. He was a big powerful man with a voice to match. About five a.m. we were called out on an accident. At a railroad crossing, a train had collided with a car carrying five people. I hadn't worked with Stockwell much, but on the way he confided that he couldn't take the sight of blood without fainting. I suggested he handle the traffic and get what information he could while I helped the injured. The car was down a ravine alongside the crossing! It was crushed with all those people inside, like an old tin can.

With the assistance of several truck drivers, we worked with crowbars and hack saws, trying to get them out. It wasn't a very pretty thing to see. From time to time, I could hear my partner's powerful voice . . . warning people not to go down. Several times I heard him repeat, "Don't go down there, lady." Then I heard him roar, "Lay there, damn you . . . I told you not to go down that bank!" Glancing up, I saw sprawled, half way down the bank, a lady in a dead faint! Stockwell, however, did allow a couple of volunteers to go down and revive her. By the time we had those five people out of that smashed car, three were dead and the other two were in mighty poor condition.

My partner, Roy Ernst, on a favorite mount.

CHAPTER 12

TEMPLE STATION

and the

SAN FRANCISCITO DAM

1927 – 1928

One day, along about the last of September, 1927, when I was on duty at the office, an order came in from the Main Office downtown for the captain. "Transfer one man to the Temple Station. Because of health problems, one of the deputies there has to be transferred to Newhall."

My captain was distraught. He said, "Who do you transfer when you have a good crew?" I don't know why, but I volunteered. Then he really blew up and wanted to know 'why, why me?' I told him that "If I were working in Temple, I could go to school in Pasadena as it was close by." My captain didn't like it one bit but he gave me the transfer.

My action was a shock to all my friends at Newhall, as well. I think I was as surprised at myself as anyone.

At Temple Station, I was just in time to get detailed to a brand new type of service. There had been a considerable number of fruit and poultry thefts in the area . . . big ones. A patrol was to be started. I believe, it was to be the first regular patrol operated by the Sheriff's Department. We could receive messages over the air but there was no way of answering them. When we received a call, we would make the investigation, then phone in our report to the station. Our first orders where to circulate and advertise . . . let everybody know that there was a patrol. My partner was Tex King, an old-timer who knew the territory. We worked from seven p.m. until three a.m.

The idea of this patrol was a good one. Thefts and other crimes in our district decreased rapidly. From then on, patrolling was a must. It wasn't long before equipment was perfected so that two way communication was possible.

One morning, about one thirty a.m., my partner and I stopped by the station. The telephone rang. Being near, I answered. It was the captain from the main office downtown. The captain reported that the San Franciscito Dam had gone out. It was March 13, 1928. The Santa Clara Valley was a disaster area and hundreds of people were reported to have drowned. He ordered me to make a log of the call, then call my captain. After that, I was to pick up a carload of Temple deputies and go to Newhall . . . they would be needing all the help they could get.

Long before daylight that morning, I reported with four other deputies to my old captain at Newhall. The four were assigned to work with Newhall crews . . . then he gave me a rundown on what happened. He detailed me to go around behind the dam and on down to Castaic. There had been no word from the other side of the Santa Clara Valley and information was needed for a report from there.

I took the route up Bouquet Canyon and cut west on mountain roads. I was thankful that I had worked that territory long enough to become familiar with it. At Castaic, the waters had not yet reached the residential areas, but were close. There was a string of cars and trucks backed up for a mile or more from the waters' edge on the Ridge Route Highway. The driver of a truck, parked at an angle across the highway there, told me that as he approached the area in the dark, he couldn't believe what he was seeing! "All the water . . . everywhere in that dry desert country." Instinctively, he had applied his brakes and his truck stopped before he was in it too deep. Two cars and a bus passed him before he could pull his rig across the road and block it! By doing what he did he, no doubt, saved many a man's life that morning! Weeks later, an overturned bus was dug out of the mud and sixteen bodies recovered.

From information I gathered, the dam went out shortly after midnight March 12, 1928. A wall of water varying from 40 to 60 feet high dashed down the narrow San Franciscito Canyon for four or five miles to the Santa Clara Valley. There, it spread out to a wave about ten feet high and traveled on for 45 or 50 miles to the ocean. It rolled right through portions of Piru, Fillmore and Santa Paula, raising havoc every foot of the way. The Ventura County Coroner's Office reported recovering 319 bodies with 101 people missing and never accounted for. Along with the bodies recovered in Los Angeles County, there was a loss of well over 500 people. My guess was that there would be perhaps three times that many head of cattle, along with many horses and sheep lost. Damage ran into the many millions of dollars.

For the next ten days, I worked doing the many difficult things peace officers have to do in times of disaster. I saw many sights that I hope I will never have to see again and I learned how people can turn out and work their darndest to help when help is needed. Those people of Newhall were great . . . they did everything they could.

Shortly after returning to Temple Station, Captain Conley put me to work as an investigator with Glenn Losey. It was interesting work and I was proud of my promotion. Investigating is the same work detectives do in the Police Departments. We handled all cases originating in our territory, right on through the courts to completion. One thing I didn't like about that job was the hours. If necessary, I had to work 24 hours a day.

Soon after returning to Temple, my first day off I went home to visit my mother and family. Monica told me a surprising thing. She and Al had made a trip to the San Franciscito Dam on Sunday, the day before the break. The keeper was a friend of Al's and they spent the entire day visiting. Monica and Al were asked, "Where are you kids going on your honeymoon?" The answer was, they didn't care about a long trip or anything like that. They'd just as soon camp in some quiet place where they would be by themselves. Al's friend, the keeper, came up with the perfect solution, "We have just the place for you. In the middle of our lake, there's a nice island, ideal for camping. I could take you and your gear out in the boat and come for you whenever you say."

That solved (they thought) their honeymoon problem.

For a wedding gift, I picked out a mantle clock that I knew Monica admired . . . but, that wasn't enough. Ever since prohibition, wine, or any kind of liquor, was not too easy to get. I managed to acquire a good supply of rabbi's sacramental wine that was appreciated by the bride and groom as well as by all the members of the wedding party!

Bill Horton, now an investigator at Temple Station, was interested in learning how to fly. An opportunity had come up and he had

178

purchased an OXX5 Jennie that he was keeping at a field in the area. Bill offered me half interest in the plane if I would teach him how to fly. I agreed and he was getting along fine. One day when we were both off duty, we flew up to Newhall. Flying over that Newhall Pass was always a rough ride and the stick on this occasion was all over the cockpit. We landed in an open field at the mouth of Placerita Canyon. It was a small but adequate place.

I hitched a ride to the Sheriff's Station. When Captain Stewart found out how I had come to Newhall, he got excited. He called his wife . . . she had always been anxious to take a ride in an airplane and this was her chance. I took her up for a nice ride. We went up over the Santa Clara Valley as far north as Castaic.

When we got back, Bill had arranged with several other people for rides at $5 each. My work was cut out for me. By the time I finished, we had earned enough to pay expenses and carry us for some time. The Stewarts had invited us for dinner, so Bill and I enjoyed a fine meal as well as a good visit. We were both supposed to be back at Temple Station that evening so we had to cut our visit short.

We returned to the plane. During our absence, the wind had changed direction and was blowing from the south. That made it necessary to take off in the direction of Newhall and directly into the rising hill country. I didn't like it, but with the wind as strong as it was, there was no other way.

We took off and cleared the first ridge between Placerita Canyon and Newhall, then as we flew over the village, the plane started settling. The motor was purring along great, but the plane wasn't going up . . . it was coming down! I started a wide, very easy turn trying to head away from the village and out over open country. The plane was in a nasty down-current! Now, we were very low and I was concerned as we dodged the tops of some very high trees . . . I failed to see a tall aerial pole sticking up above a house. My lower right wing ripped through the cable guy line to that pole and it cut a slot in the leading edge of the lower wing. It finally hung up on an insulator that had broken free from its attachment to the ground. The plane acted as if it had been lassoed on the tip of the wing. It went into a twisting whirl and cork-screwed down through a huge umbrella tree to the ground! The shock of the crash was absorbed with hardly a jolt to Bill and I.

In nothing flat, my safety belt was released and I jumped to the ground! The house had been hit by one of our whirling wings but recieved very little damage. Two girls came running out of the front door. The older one shouted "Hello Paul!" I answered "Hello Stella!" (Stella was a student nurse at the General Hospital. Marion and I had gone out with Stella and Roy. What a heck of a way to drop in on a friend). Then I turned to see why Bill hadn't departed the plane. There he was, in the cockpit, sitting and looking at one of his hands! He had grabbed the exaust pipe as he started to get out! I yelled, "Get out of there, Bill, before it starts to burn! JUMP!" Bill jumped!

When I looked back towards the girls, Stella's young sister had fainted and was lying on the front steps. About this time the usual curious crowd of people was arriving to see the sights. As Bill and I were trying to revive the poor girl on the steps, I heard one old gal in our sight-seeing crowd say, "Serves her right for going up in that thing!"

CHAPTER 13

WEST HOLLYWOOD

1928 – 1929

One morning, at Temple Station, I was surprised by a visit from Bill Hanby, my friend from the Sheriff's Cattle Theft Detail. We visited for awhile, then he asked me to come out to his car. There, he asked me why I hadn't put in for the new station that was to be opened in West Hollywood? I told him that, "I was doing alright where I was and that I probably couldn't get to Hollywood if I wanted. There were already supposedly 40 or 50 requests in for that "prize" post. What chance would I have?"

Then Bill said, "If you knew that I was going to be the captain there, would that make any difference?

"Sure, if your'e going to be the captain there, it would make all the difference in the world. I most certainly would like to work for you!"

Several days later, I was transferred to the Hollywood station in time for its opening, July 23, 1928. The station at first was called Sherman Station. Perhaps because it took in the

Sherman District bordering Beverly Hills. Our area was like an island of un-incorporated territory surrounded by Beverly Hills, Los Angeles and Hollywood. It was located on Fairfax Avenue just north of Santa Monica Blvd., in the approximate center of what is known as West Hollywood.

At Sherman Station, we answered calls from un-incorporated areas as far away as Malibu and Calabasas. West Hollywood was heavily populated and our calls from there, for the most part, were more urban than the usual calls recieved at either Newhall or Temple.

For a time, I worked with Russ Bowman. He was a sort of playboy and loved the Hollywood life. Trouble was, he never got over it and our partnership didn't last long. I'll never forget one night, we were working the evening shift and got a disturbance call. A wild party with too much noise. When we arrived, we found a good sized crowd of young people having a ball. The owner of that property was told to quiet them down. He took it well and complied. As we were leaving, he invited Russ and I to come back after we got off shift and have some fun. I didn't think it was such a good idea but Russ wanted to go, so we went.

When we arrived, our host appeared pleased and safely parked our "hardware." There was a large room being used for dancing and the orchestra was good. I asked a young lady to dance and she accepted. We were doing fine until we danced by a group of people. As we passed, I felt the impact of a kick she had received! Trying to avoid trouble, we headed for the far side of the room, but the fellow who had kicked her followed. He pulled us apart and took a swing at me but missed. I took a swing at him and didn't miss! Next thing you know, we were both down in the middle of the room going round and round . . . a first class wrestling match! Then, my fun-loving partner started pulling me off from on top of this fellow; saying, "Come on Paul, we better get out of here!"

As our host was giving us back our guns, he said, "I saw that play from the start. I'm glad that fellow finally got just what was coming to him. I'm sorry you fellows have to leave in such a hurry."

I had several weeks vacation time coming, so I invited my 15 year old brother. Bill, to go on a camping trip with me. Bill was on his summer vacation from school. We loaded up my Ford roadster and headed north. Bill had never driven a car on his own, but, like all young people, was anxious to learn. When we had made our way over the ridge, I became tired and sleepy. I let Bill take over the driving and when I woke up some time later that morning, we were well north of the Merced turn-off to Yosemite Valley. I told Bill, "Since you missed that turn off, guess we'll have to go all the way to Portland." For awhile, I'm sure he felt that his failure to make that turn was why we went all the way to Portland.

You, no doubt, know who I contacted first when we arrived in Portland . . . Katherine! While I was enjoying myself, Bill had the opportunity to visit his old friends. Trouble was, our vacation time ran out too fast. But when Bill and I took off for our return trip, Katherine and I were engaged to be married!

An interesting thing happened when I went to purchase Katherine's engagement ring. Katherine and I had a friend in Portland, who happened to be a jewler. I went to him and selected a very nice ring. When we were talking price, payment, etc., my friend casually asked who the ring was for. When I told him "Katherine," he said, "Oh, no! I thought I had a sale . . . but I guess this isn't my lucky day."

I asked him what he meant by that and he

answered, "Twice before, others had bought rings for her . . . then in a few days they would bring them back and beg out of the deal."

I didn't have to bring <u>my</u> ring back!

Shortly after we returned to Sherman Station, I was working with Shelly Walton, an old time Marshall. We received an accident call on Santa Monica Boulevard in Sherman. When we arrived, we found nothing but an old beat-up car with a large woman wedged down forward of the front passenger seat. Boy was she drunk! Shelly said, "If this old clunker will run, I'll drive it to the station and we'll have some help unloading."

Shelley got in, stepped on the starter and took off. I followed. At the first signal, Shelley had to stop. He put his foot on the brake but nothing happened . . . there wasn't any! That old crate smashed into the back of a very nice car that had stopped ahead of him. The old wreck had no bumper . . . just two angle irons sticking out in front where a bumper was supposed to be attached. Those angle irons ran right through the gas tank of the car ahead and the gas ran into the street! Stopping behind Shelley, I got out and went to help. As I walked ahead, Shelley passed me on his way back to the sheriff's car muttering, "You tell him Paul . . . don't think I better."

Only after telling that infuriated driver and showing him what was in the front seat of the wreck did he calm down. However, it took a tow truck to clear the mess.

A cooperative Justice of the Peace, along with the involved insurance companies, were able to come up with a satisfactory solution to our problem.

Once, I was working with Glenn Packer on the evening shift. We got a call . . . "Disturbance at the El Trocadero," one of the dining show places of Hollywood. When we arrived, we were met outside by the manager. A drunk had taken over the stage and was threatening everybody with a pistol. No one knew the man, nor did anyone know whether or not the gun was loaded. Needless to say, that man had a captive audience. He had given an order that no one was to leave that cafe! Glenn suggested that the manager open up the back door and let me in while he made his approach from the front. The manager did as my partner suggested and I silently made my way to the stage.

This "ham" was really entertaining those people! As I carefully came closer to him, Glenn walked right down the isle and up to the stage. He stopped and put his foot up on the two-foot high edge of the platform, acting like he was tying his shoe, and started talking to this fellow. The man really had a pistol in his hand and with it, was emphasizing the points he was making. By that time, I was directly behind him. Glenn nodded his head and made a grab for the gun arm! I got a bear hold on him from the back! You should have heard that audience yell and applaud! Our play worked like we had practiced and practiced. The audience had been held for well over a half hour, not knowing whether that fellow would carry out his threat. It turned out that the gun was loaded!

Ever since my vacation, several times a week, Katherine and I had been exchanging letters. Finally, the time arrived for me to go north and get my bride. I sent Katherine the telegram she was awaiting. It was a thursday when I arrived in Portland and we planned to be married on saturday. The excitement and preparations were pretty tough on her. Her brother Frank had to go with me to get the license.

January 10, 1929, was clear and cold. Father Daley performed the marriage in Saint Mary's Church in Albina. Katherine and I had been born in Albina and we were both baptized in that very same church. Katherine's sister, Margaret, was the bridesmaid and her brother, Frank, was the best man. Our nephews, John and Bob Danaher, served mass.

After the wedding breakfast, we celebrated with our relatives and friends. In the late afternoon, we boarded the Sunset Limited and were on our way south. We stopped in San Francisco at the Saint Francis Hotel and spent our honeymoon there.

King Collins had been my partner when I left Hollywood and I had confided in him. He had offered to pick Katherine and I up at the Los Angeles depot and transport us to our new home. Sure enough, upon our arrival at the depot, there was King, standing alongside one of those huge concrete columns in the middle of a big crowd. I had been carrying our two large suitcases, Katherine was carrying the two smaller ones. As we walked up to King, I set my suitcases down and shook his hand. When I turned to introduce Katherine, SHE WAS GONE! She had completely disappeared in the large crowd. I looked frantically here and there and started to fuss and fume. Then I glanced at King and saw that silly grin on his face. I knew he was in on something and I was just about ready to jump him, when he volunteered, "Come on Paul, calm down . . . I might know just where your wife disappeared to."

We carried the baggage out to the front of the depot and there, two large County Cadillacs (Sheriff's cars) were parked. Each one was full of West Hollywood deputies. In the back seat of the most crowded car, wedged in between all those guys, was Katherine. That crew had kidnapped her from me in the crowded Los Angeles depot. Looking back, I wasn't surprised. Among them were some of the cleverest fellows I have ever known. King said, "No room for us in that car, Paul. We better

Crew in front of the Sherman (West Hollywood)
Station the day it opened, July 23, 1928.

The house on Fountain Avenue in West Hollywood
where Katherine and I first lived after our
marriage. Katherine and Johnnie are standing
alongside our Ford.

jam into the other one."

With red lights flashing and sirens wailing, both cars took off . . . down through Los Angeles, out Wilshire Boulevard, all the way to Fairfax and north to the station. I'm sure Katherine never had such a ride in all her life!

Awaiting us at the station was Captain and Mrs. Hanby, a good many of the other deputies and their wives, and other friends. They welcomed us with a first class party. Very few young couples have ever had a more exciting or thrilling "welcome back" from their honeymoon. After the party was over, we were taken to our new home . . . a duplex on Florence Avenue within easy walking distance from the station.

The California Motor Vehicle Division had called in all old drivers' licenses, as new, more modern ones were being issued. However, to secure one, a driving test was necessary. All Police and Sheriff's Departments were cooperating in the issuing of these licenses. I was working days and we were busy.

One day, a glamorous starlett stopped by to get her license. She was driving a big fancy car and I went with her for her driving test. We weren't gone long, but just guess who had walked to the station (for the first time) to surprise me? You guessed it! It was Katherine! When I got out of the car where I had been sitting alongside that pretty girl, Katherine didn't say a word. The look she gave, however, was something else!! That wasn't my lucky day.

Roy Ernst, my old side-kick from Newhall, was now working at the San Dimas Station. He and I were still making trips on our days off to the mountains southwest of Mt. Frazier. We had been prospecting there for placer gold as well as the gold's hard rock source. It was our "excuse" to get to the mountains we both loved. We had erected a lean-to there and had made it into a "sort of" permanent camp. Katherine didn't like the two mile climb up the mountain but once on top, she was thrilled! She even got a kick out of our lean-to. That country, especially from there, was beautiful! Most every day, we would see deer, quail and grouse, but, you did have to watch out for rattlesnakes. The place was so remote that we hardly ever encountered a stranger, even during the deer hunting season.

Roy and I had discovered some placer gold, but the water for sluicing was scarse. In the winter, though, there were times when we did have plenty. It was thrilling to recover even a small nugget!

During the flu epidemic when my nephew, Bob, was only a few weeks old, his mother, Phyrn (my sister), passed away. The responsibility of raising Johnnie and Bob shifted primarily to John Senior's parents, the Danahers, and on occasion, to the Nesters. Having been bounced around a lot, Johnnie needed a break. Katherine and I offered our home to him and he accepted. Johnnie, however, turned out to be quite a problem. Immediately after coming to live with us, he started testing our authority. It took some time for him to learn, but he finally came around to respecting and abiding by our rules.

Meanwhile, back at the office, business was growing rapidly. It was decided that another team of investigators was needed. Al Guasti and I were appointed. Al had been raised in Los Angeles and knew the city well. He had a lot of friends in the Hollywood area and, as a team, we worked well together.

Early one winter morning, I got a telephone call from Captain Hanby. The day before, an airplane on its way from Bakersfield to Los Angeles, had disappeared in the mountains south of Mt. Frazier. Frank Dewar, the Los Angeles County Undersheriff and eight other passengers were aboard. I was ordered to go to

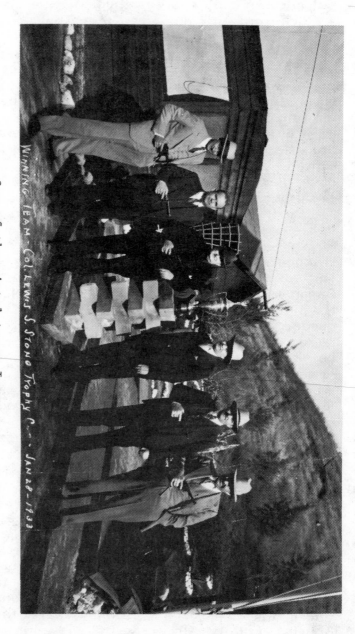

One of the pistol teams I was on.
(From left--Paul Nester, Al Guasti,
Colonel Hotz, Captain Bill Hanby,
Jay Morley and Walter Keating.)

Winning Team-Col.Lewis S.Stone Trophy (~~Jan 28-1933)

Newhall and join a search party that was assembling there. Within an hour or two, fully outfitted in winter gear, I reported at the Newhall Station.

Two forestry trucks, loaded with supplies and a string of pack mules and saddle horses were ready and waiting. Soon, my old partner, Roy Ernst, showed up with several forestry officers I didn't know. We all proceeded up the Ridge Route Road, passed Gorman and then turned west on the Hungry Valley road. The trucks took us through two or three inches of snow, as far as they could go. Transferring to the saddle horses and pack mules, we proceeded on up the Alimo mountain. Our destination was the Baker Cabin, eighteen miles up the trail.

Leonard Secenia, a forestry officer friend of mine, was in charge of the saddle horses and the string of six mules. As we climbed the mountain, the snow kept getting deeper and deeper. When we finally reached the Baker Cabin, the snow was sixteen to eighteen inches deep and the animals were having a time of it.

We got the packs and supplies unloaded, including pairs of snowshoes and skis for each man, when Leonard shouted, "I've got to get these animals down before dark. I'll be back for you in about a week. FIND THAT PLANE."

All five of us, three forestry officers and two deputy sheriffs, had been selected for this job for two reasons: we knew the mountains in that area and we had the ability to take care of ourselves in the winter under survival conditions.

No time was lost getting wood chopped and a fire started. The cabin hadn't been used for quite a while so we all pitched in and cleaned it up. After supper, we laid plans for our operations. Each man would take his turn, stay at the cabin, do the cooking, chop wood and keep things ship-shape. I'll tell you, it sure

191

paid to be a good cook. By the time we left, I was sure, each man there was, indeed, a good cook.

We had two search teams, each made up of a forestry officer and a deputy sheriff. Good maps of the area made it possible to plan each day's work. If it didn't snow, we would be able to cover the area in a week. We would try to do all our traveling on the ridges, avoiding the canyons. Deep snow was only one of the dangers.

Each morning we were up and had a good breakfast before daylight. We tried to utilize every daylight hour. One day during a lunch break, my partner and I were relaxing. I needed to adjust the tyings on my snowshoes, so I had taken them off. Suddenly the crust of the snow broke and I went through! As I went down, I was able to grab one of my snowshoes . . . that saved me! I didn't know how deep the snow in that drift was, but I was down in it full length and couldn't feel anything solid. I was mighty thankful I had a partner to help get me out.

On the sixth day, along about ten o'clock in the morning, we heard our pre-arranged signal (a series of shots fired) which told us to return to the cabin.

Leonard and his partner, with the saddle horses and pack mules, were there. He brought word that the plane had been discovered. It had crashed in a ravine on the south side of Mt. Frazier and all aboard had lost their lives! The bodies were being hauled out. It was time for us to pack up and leave. Within an hour we were on our way and I was back home that night, happy but tired.

By now, I had passed three rating steps in the Sheriff's Office and was up for the fourth. I had taken the Civil Service examination for Senior Deputy Sheriff and had passed fourth on the list. One day I was called

downtown to the Undersheriff's office. My first
meeting with the Undersheriff was
disappointing. He opened the interview about
like this: "I don't know you Nester, but the
Sheriff insists that you get this promotion."
Then he went on to tell me how good a man his
friend who had passed number five on that list
was. I don't know why, but that's one man I
never did like and I had the feeling it was
mutual.

Katherine, Margaret Ann and I in
front of the cabin we rented on
the beach.

Swimming with Margaret Ann when
she was a little over one year old.

CHAPTER 14

TOPANGA OUTPOST

1930 – 1932

Back at the station, Captain Hanby called me into his office. He told me that the new Sheriff's Outpost, which was being built out on the coast at the mouth of Topanga Canyon, was nearing completion. Four deputies would be stationed there and would handle all business originating in the Malibu and Calabasas townships. The Outpost would be operated under the West Hollywood Station's jurisdiction. He asked if I would be interested in taking charge there. Surprised and very pleased, I accepted.

When I told Katherine, she was just as happy as I. Right away, we started looking for a new home, reasonably close to Topanga. We were fortunate . . . we found one in the Pacific Palisades. It was a home with only one other house in the block and was like living out in the country.

The day Topanga Outpost opened, Ed Adams, Frank Cannon, Tommie Thompson and I were transferred there. Each man would be working alone on an eight hour shift. Every fifth day, he would have a day off and I would do the relieving. On my extra day, I would do the investigating and take care of any other business. The schedule was set up so I would relieve the two night men in one sixteen hour shift. Arranged with my regular day off, that made a good break for me. Katherine liked it too.

It took a while to get used to the territory. Over twenty one miles along the coast, the road ran through Rincon Range property . . . an old Spanish Land Grant. It has been said, the owners, Mrs. Rincon and her family, had fought (right up to the Supreme Court) to keep the highway from being built through their property. They lost because the road was probably considered to be a military necessity. The Rincon fighting spirit though was still there.

It also has been said that when the State finally won the right to construct the road, another thing happened to upset the Rincon's. Mrs. Rincon refused to accept the offer the State had made for the land appropriated for the right-of-way. She was asked what, in her opinion, the land was worth. She mentioned a large sum. The State paid her that sum, but thereafter, when her land was appraised for tax purposes, it all was appraised at her assessment. The high taxes came close to causing disaster.

Soon therafter, the Mandell Land Company, a family corporation, was formed. Very valuable land was probably put on the market much sooner than it would otherwise have been. The result was the very rapid growth of Malibu which took in all the Rincon property along the coast line from Los Flores to Ventura County.

The Rincon people also had trouble with "squatters." A bit of misinformation which led many people to believe that Spanish Land Grants could be broken by staking out and holding property by force if necessary, had been circulated. It was surprising how many people fell for this false information. For a period of time, it was necessary for the sheriffs at least once a day, to patrol the coast road to the Ventura County line. Our job was to observe. The "squatters" usually came in groups, and if we spotted any, our orders were to call for help.

One time we were confronted by a group of nearly fifty people. They were armed and ready to stake claims on Rincon property. I was with a group of ten deputies. There was also a group of about ten Rincon Range cowboys. Things got so tense there for awhile, I thought that if someone had accidentally set off a firecracker, a dozen people would have been killed.

The Rincon fighting spirit carried over to their ranch help. Their cowboys took great pleasure in kicking people off property they considered theirs . . . in particular, the beaches. Many a row would start up and have to be resolved.

Just to show how the deputies got along with the Rincon employees, one day Frank Cannon was making a patrol up to the county line. He stopped to take care of a "call of nature." Getting out of his car, Frank went down into a gully, out of sight. As he was returning, Vander, the big six foot two Rincon foreman drove up in a car with his wife. When Frank came up to his car, Vander demanded to know what he was doing down there. Always a gentleman, Frank identified himself and said he wasn't doing any damage to the property. Vander wasn't satisfied and became very demanding. He wanted an explanation. Out of respect for the lady, Frank avoided a direct answer . . . but since Vander insisted, Frank told him in plain words just what he had been doing, adding, "Now I feel much better, thank you." With that, he took his leave.

The cabin I built in 1932 and lived in until
the 1938 fire.

After the fire.

One day I was working the day shift alone. An excited man rushed into the station and said, "There's trouble at the Topanga Spring!" Two and a half miles up Topanga there's a spring where people got very good drinking water free for the taking. On a busy day, a half dozen or more cars would be lined up with people waiting their turn to fill their bottles. Usually everybody was patient and cooperative.

When I arrived, I was informed that there had been the usual line of people awaiting their turn. A big guy pulled up in his car, took a five gallon bottle and walked to the spring. He removed the bottle that was under the faucet and put his bottle in its place. Everybody there was upset but this big fellow didn't give a damn. The owner of the partially filled bottle was a little fellow so he didn't say a word but he went to his car, got a pistol, returned and put a bullet through the big man's bottle! The little fellow's bottle was now full and he appeared to be in charge.

I checked to see if the little man had a permit to carry a gun and he did. The big fellow didn't like it but, rather than being arrested for disturbing the peace, he cleaned up the glass (that had once been his bottle) and Topanga Spring resumed business as usual.

My mother came out to our home in the Pacific Palisades to sort of look after Johnnie when Katherine and I made our first vacation trip home to Portland since our marriage. When we returned, we were surprised and disappointed. During our absence, Johnnie had refused to obey mother and had done just as he pleased. When I reprimanded him, he told me he was going to continue doing "just as he pleased."

Katherine and I both felt Johnnie's father should be advised, so Katherine wrote him a letter. Soon thereafter, Johnnie received an invitation from his father to come and live in

New York. In just a few days, Johnnie was on his way.

It wasn't long after that when Katherine wrote to Portland and invited Bob, Johnnie's younger brother, to come live with us. He was pleased. From then until he graduated from Santa Monica High school in June 1939, our home was his. By that Fall, before school started, Bob had joined the U.S. Marines.

Driving to and from work along the coast road, I passed a fine location where there once had been a house. I could picture a home there now. If placed right, it would close off the entrance to a ravine and give the owner the privacy of a beautiful canyon that ran well back into the mountains. One could have an outstanding view of the ocean all the way from Topanga to Santa Monica.

The next time I met Mr. Guy Ware, manager for the Tide Insurance and Trust Company, owners of land, I talked about that lot. Mr. Ware was friendly and I made a deal . . . I would build my home there and it would be within one half mile of Topanga where I worked.

I went to work building my own home, and for the next year, all my spare time was put in working on it. On his days off, Al Shaw, my brother-in-law, helped me as much as he could. Even though our home was far from being finished, Katherine and I, along with Bob, moved in before the year was over.

One evening in 1932, a young man stopped by the Outpost and wanted to know if there was an old barn in the area where he could sleep. In that area, there were no barns and we badly needed something like that . . . remember . . . these were depression times . . . many people were without homes and had a hard time finding food to eat. I had made an arrangement with the lady owner of a nearby cafe that if I sent anyone there to eat, she would feed them. The regular price for a fine big meal was 25¢ but it only cost me 12½¢. When I found out how long it had been since this young fellow had eaten, I sent him over for a meal. When he returned, I found a place for him to sleep in the Outpost. The next morning I took him home and Katherine fixed a breakfast.

He told me his name was Al Pelath and he was 19 years old. He had come to the west coast all the way from the east. He said his father was a carpenter and a building contractor and claimed to be a carpenter as well. I put him to work and, very soon, was satisfied that he knew his trade. Al did all the finish carpentry on our cabin. He was happy to have work and it suited me fine as I was very, very tired.

Our Outpost had been built on a steep hillside and underneath there was a large area that could be enclosed. I was able to scrape up some used lumber so Al went to work enclosing that space. When he was finished, we had a good sized room and there was also another one large enough to bed down six or eight hungry, homeless men. You have no idea how many times that room was full to capacity for overnight.

One winter day, I was working alone at the Outpost. We had been having unusual weather. It was very cold and it had been raining. Snow had fallen and the tops of the Santa Monica mountains were partially covered. A car pulled up in front and stopped. A man, all excited, ran in and reported a burglar in his cabin up in the Fernwood District, about five miles away. He offered to take me there, but I took my car instead. On the way up the grade, he told me he owned a cabin at the end of a remote road. His family used that cabin on weekends, and on this day he had gone up to get some things they had forgotten on their last trip. As he came into view of his place, he noticed a car parked in front. Stopping, he observed a man going in and coming out of the cabin carrying objects to his car. Right then, he decided he better get some help.

We drove as close as we could to the cabin without being seen and parked. Sure enough, the stranger's car was still there. As we walked towards the cabin, the man must have seen us. He ran to his car, jumped in and headed down the road. I tried to stop him but even with my .44 in my hand, he didn't stop. He tried to run me down but I jumped off the edge of the road! As his car started around a curve where it would be out of sight, I took a shot at his gas tank. We ran back to my car and began following. There was just enough snow and mud to follow his tracks. By fortunate chance, the fellow turned onto mountain roads instead of getting back on the main highway. Finally, we caught up to his car, stalled in a mud puddle.

The burglar was standing off to one side. I got out and told him he was under arrest for burglary. While covering him with my .44, I commanded him to put his hands up. He told me to "Go to Hell!" I gave my handcuffs to the victim and told him to see if he could put them on. As the victim, (a little fellow) approached, the burglar squared off and told him to "get out!" The victim came back and handed my handcuffs to me. I asked him if he could handle a pistol? He said he had served in the army and was familiar with small arms. I gave him my .44 and told him to use it only if he had to.

Taking my handcuffs I approached the man. He was bigger and heavier than I and, as I approached, he squared off like a professional. This, however, was not to be a boxing match . . . all too soon, it turned into an all-out "free for all." I was able to get the cuffs on one of his wrists, but was having a heck of a time getting the other secured. Then, all of a sudden, my opponent went limp and I was able to complete handcuffing him. The victim informed me that he finally had the chance to smack that burglar on the back of his head with my .44! I was sure thankful for his help.

The burglar's car was loaded with the victim's property. Later, I found out why he didn't want to be captured . . . he was already a three time loser, and in the state of California, a four time loser (upon conviction) automatically goes to the state prison for the rest of his life.

One evening I was working the four to twelve shift. Along about ten o'clock, I got a call. There was a bad fire at the Malibu Beach Film Colony. The Fire Department had already been notified. Upon my arrival three two-story houses were ablaze and the fire department was already pumping water. A strong wind was blowing from the west, endangering a long row of two-story houses, built close to each other. The fire department needed a lot more help than they had. The fire captain informed me that help was coming from other County fire companies and that the Santa Monica Fire Department had also promised to help.

We were worried that some of those houses might have people in them. I went to the fourth house and rang the door bell, made a lot of noise and then broke in. I searched each and every room for sleepers, drunks, or what have you! When I came out, that house was on fire. I broke in and searched each and every house as the fire continued to advance! As each house started to burn, I was breaking in and searching the house next door! Finally, when I was at the twelfth house, I had to haul three drunks out! My idea had been good. If it hadn't been for me, they might not have made it.

Fifteen houses burned to the ground that night and there would have been more if the fire department hadn't dynamited house number sixteen! That gave them a clearing of sorts and from there the fire faced a wall of water! The line held there! For weeks, my shoulders and back were sore.

About this time, they started sending more deputies to work at the Outpost. The personnel was gradually built up until I had two men on each watch and a relief man for their days off. Now, I was working days.

Topanga was the only Outpost they had in the County. I found out that nearly every man that was transferred there was kicked out of some station because the captain of that station didn't want them. I found out too, that all these men were good officers. On occasion, they might disregard some of the department's petty rules or regulations, but at work, they did a good job. They had more guts than the average deputy and I knew if it came to real trouble, they were the kind of men I wanted with me. I never ever had occasion to transfer any one of them.

Paul Nester and the Malibu Constable
in front of our brand new Outpost.

CHAPTER 15

MALIBU STATION

1933 - 1935

For some time, the Justice of Peace of Malibu Township, had been dissatisfied with the quarters used for his Justice Court. He got busy and the result was a very fine Spanish-type brick building, large enough for the Court House and a Sheriff's Station as well. When it was completed, the Topanga Outpost was shut down and its personnel transferred to the new station which thereafter was called the Malibu Outpost. The location, on the Coast Highway at Los Flores, was excellent. We were all proud of our new station.

One thing we did miss though, was the facility for taking care of homeless men on cold winter nights. That problem, however, was soon solved by using the plush, warm court room. Our travelers had to stay quiet and keep out of sight. This was not difficult for them, they usually were very tired. Each morning by six o'clock, they were roused out and would be on their way. . . As far as I know, neither the Judge nor any of the authorities ever knew about this. We were afraid that if they found out, they would put an end to it fast.

Ed Adams was working the midnight to eight a.m. shift. One night when he was on his way to work, he observed what appeared to be an unusual situation. There had been a series of hold-ups of people in parked cars along the coast. Ed investigated and caught a stick-up man right in the act! That man was disarmed, searched, handcuffed and taken to his car where a woman was waiting. She was also arrested and the pair were brought to the station. . . I was immediately notified and went to the station. Information we obtained called for further investigation and the crew was dispatched on this errand. . . The stick-up man had been booked and was in the lock-up. The woman was sitting in the office while I was typing up the log. No one else was in the station. All of a sudden I had the feeling, "Watch her". Turning, I saw her drawing a .32 automatic from between her breasts! . . . I jumped, hit her fast and hard, then disarmed her. After thoroughly searching her, she was put in the lock-up along with her pal. . . Ed's efforts that night, along with the follow-up, brought an end to a whole series of hold-ups along the coast.

Along about 1933, the Los Angeles County Sheriff's Department underwent a major change. The force became a semi-military outfit. Uniforms were adopted and every man had to purchase one for himself. . . I had passed the Lieutenant's examination number four on the list and was next up for appointment. I was ordered to get a Lieutenant's uniform. . . Most of the deputies didn't like this change and neither did I, but there was nothing one could do about it. Along with the uniforms came a lot of petty regulations which took some time to get used to.

Lee King, a retired New York Life Insurance salesman, who was a friend, had a nice home about a mile up Los Flores Canyon. Lee had 'Burger's Disease' He had already lost one leg and the foot off his other leg. He was confined to a wheel chair.

One time, there was a fire in the Santa Monica mountains. As the fire approached Los Flores Canyon, the Fire Department ordered the area vacated. On his way out, Lee and his wife stopped by the station and gave their special toot on the car's horn. I went out and talked with them. Lee asked me as a favor to keep an eye on his place . . . Lee had hobbies . . . he kept bees and had a hot-house full of beautiful begonias. He loved his home and I knew what it meant to him. I gave him my promise.

Within a few days, that fire had swept through and was well beyond the Los Flores Canyon. I made a trip up and came into the Los Flores canyon from a back road. There had been many homes in that canyon and my heart sank as I came into view of the devastation . . . There was, however, a group of three houses that hadn't been touched by the fire. I made my way to Lee's place. Not a bit of damage had been done to his home. I arranged water for his bees and gave the begonias a good soaking. When I returned to the office, I gave Lee a call on the phone and told him his place was okay. Lee said, "Yes, I know." I was surprised to find that someone had already informed him and asked who gave him the information. He answered, "George told me." I thought George must be a fireman so let it go at that.

Some days later, Lee and his wife stopped by on their way home. I was curious about George and asked Lee just who he was? Lee answered, "George is my Guardian Angel . . . I prayed hard that my house would be spared. . . George told me, 'Don't worry, your house is okay.'" After seeing the great majority of those houses in that canyon completely wiped out, . . . that sure made me think.

Another one of the winning teams I was on.

On November 25, 1934, in the Hollywood Hospital, Katherine gave birth to Margaret Ann, our first daughter. She was a very healthy and lively little girl and she was beautiful. Katherine and I had been hoping, praying and planning for this for a long time and we were very very happy. . . Back in those days, it was the habit of the doctors to try and keep the mother and baby in the hospital for a week or ten days. Katherine and Margaret Ann were there for just one week. How proud I was when I finally was able to bring my gals home!

Relatives and friends had already held several parties for Katherine and we had all kinds of baby clothes and supplies. Even the Judge's wife at Los Flores had given a party and I remember bringing home from there a very nice basinette. Katherine and I thought we were busy before, but after Margaret Ann arrived, the time went by so fast, I hardly know where it went.

From our front porch, we had a magnificent view. We could see most everything that happened on the ocean for many miles. Just west of the mouth of Topanga Canyon, there was an underwater rock reef which ran out a half mile or more into the ocean. In the lee of that reef, there was calmer water which gave smaller boats protection from storms. Boat owners for many miles around took advantage of this free anchorage . . . and they used it as long as they wanted. This was before the Santa Monica breakwater was built.

Sometimes, especially in the fall, when early storms would hit the coast, boats not properly secured would tear away from their moorings. They would drift with the tide and prevailing winds for a mile and a half or so, then would smash to pieces on Castle Rock point.

Bob, my nephew, and I loved to swim. Every time we saw a boat adrift, there was a challenge: "Swim out and save that boat." We would try and intercept the drifter and bring it in through the breakers onto a nice, sandy beach. Experience taught us that many of these drifters were without oars. Bringing a boat in through the surf without oars was quite a problem. So we improved our act and when we could, each of us would take an oar or a paddle out with us. I believe this was the sport Bob liked best during his High School days. For me, every time I got a chance to do it, it was a thrill.

One day, when Bob was not home, Jerry Tabnac, a neighbor, came over. He had spotted a boat adrift and wanted me to go out with him and help save that boat. Jerry owned a small rowboat and was expert at handling it in the surf. We made it through the breakers and out to the drifter, even though the waves were extremely high that day. It was a sail boat, much larger than I had ever brought in before. I doubted my ability to bring her in through those breakers. I only had a paddle with me. However, Jerry helped me. We rowed and towed that drifter for over an hour . . . finally getting lined up properly to make the run in. Then Jerry gave me his oars and he took my paddle. He brought his boat in okay.

I maneuvered until I could pick the proper wave, then went all out to get that boat to crest at the right time. I was lucky, everything went all right. That sailboat rode the crest of that wave like a surfboard . . . all the way!

It was a holiday and there were a lot of people on the beach. When I stepped out of the boat, high up on the sandy beach, those people gave me a cheer that was my second big surprise and delight of that day.

Driving to and from Santa Monica, I had noticed an old dory on the beach near the Lighthouse Cafe. Now, there was a "For Sale" sign on that dory. I stopped, looked it over, went in and inquired about the price. When I came out, I was the owner of that boat. It was transported home and I got started on the overhaul and rebuilding I planned for it. It took a couple of months, but I converted that dory into an adjustible steel center-board sailor. Jerry helped me lay out the sails and we rigged that boat perfectly.

For anchorage, a permanent moorage was arranged directly out in front of our house. A heavy old motor was picked up at a junk yard. A chain was shackled to this motor, allowing for a 25 to 30 foot water depth. An old oil drum was secured to the chain which would act as a tying up buoy. Getting all that heavy equipment out through the surf and in place 200 yards or so off shore wasn't easy.

One day, when the breakers were especially low, we launched my pride and joy. It sailed beautifully and I was very happy with it. Only thing now was, in order to sail, I had to swim out to the boat. Needless to say, most all my trips were alone. On occasion however, I did have company. But they did have to make their way out through the surf where I could pick them up. Trolling for barracuda was what I liked doing best.

On several occasions when I was out sailing alone, a heavy fog would come in and I was unable to see the shore line. It sort of reminded me of the time I was flying a Jennie along the coast west of Santa Monica. Sailing a dory, however, was a lot safer. You could hear the sound of traffic and other land noises. The roar of the surf crashing on a rocky point could be recognized and used as a guide.

As time went by, I discovered that my anchorage was a good place to catch fish. So I kept fishing tackle out in the boat. All I had to do was swim out with some bait and fish. When Margaret Ann was just a very little girl, as she played on the front porch, she could see when I made a catch. I would hold the fish up and,

Personnel of the West Hollywood Station and the Malibu Outpost.

all excited, she would call her mother. Getting those fish back ashore slowed me down. It was a tow job . . . I would loop a line around my shoulder. That worked all right until the day I caught a nice big lobster. That fellow grabbed onto a rock just as I started in through the breakers. I lost my whole string that day.

Al Shaw, my brother in law, was a friend of Lee King. Lee had been helping Al get started keeping bees. Al lived in Los Angeles and there was no chance of him keeping his bees there. So I told Al to bring the bees out to my place and put them up in the canyon back of our house. Al was happy about this. Now he would really learn beekeeping. I didn't realize then, that I too would become interested in this hobby. Now, for over a third of a century, I have been harvesting the "honey rewards" one gets from the keeping of bees.

One hot, dry sunday, I was doing some work at the station when the crew, two of my largest men, brought in another very big and belligerent man. He had refused to sign a ticket. They explained what had happened: The usual sunday crowds jammed the Old Coast Road which ran by the Malibu Beach Film Colony. Cars were forced to travel slowly. That road was narrow with a lot of dust on the sides. A large car, traveling fast, passed everybody on the right edge of the road stirring up a cloud of dust. When the car stopped, the driver said, "I am the Presiding Judge of the Superior Court in Los Angeles and I am in a hurry." The crew didn't believe him and made a joke of it. Jack said, "Well, I'm King George and meet my partner, the Prince of Wales." This really made that man mad and he refused to sign a ticket! He wound up at the station.

There, he identified himself beyond any doubt. He was the Presiding Judge. When I suggested he sign the ticket so that he could proceed on his way, it made him madder than

213

ever. Finally, he did simmer down, signed the ticket and departed.

Eventually, that Judge paid his $5.00 fine and the incident was forgotten . . . OR WAS IT? . . . ?

When Bob was a freshman at Santa Monica High, one afternoon he failed to return from school. I checked with the school bus driver and was informed that Bob had not boarded the bus after school that day. That was not unusual. Often, the boys would stay after school to see a game or take part in some of the sports. When it was time to go home, they would walk over to the Boulevard stop at the base of the California Incline and hitch a ride. Most of the Topanga and Malibu people knew the kids and they had no trouble getting rides.

Bob was always home in time for supper. When he didn't show up, I gave the sheriff's office a call. They informed me that two other reports on boys not showing up after school had already come in. I took a ride up to the office and contacted the parents of these boys. They didn't know any more than I did. Neither family thought that their boy would just up and run away. So an "All Points Bulletin" on three missing boys was put out over the teletype.

A lot of worrying was done by three different families right up until about nine o'clock the next evening. Then, I received a telephone company inquiry: "Would I accept charges from a Bob Danaher in San Francisco?"

Bob was tired, hungry and broke. He told me he and his two friends had stayed after school to watch a game. After that, they walked to their usual spot to hitch a ride. A large truck transporting automobiles made the stop. On a dare, those three boys climbed up and into one of the cars. When they passed Topanga and Malibu, that truck was making thirty or forty miles per hour. Their first stop was Santa Barbara. Those boys knew that hitch-hiking back from Santa Barbara after dark would be near impossible. So they decided to stay inside the car and find out where that truck was going . . . they found out . . . San Francisco!

That day they wandered all over looking for jobs. They found out how tough it can be during depression times. They also found out how hungry one can get.

I arranged to send money for food and for their transportation back home. Two days later, all three of those boys were back home. What a story they had to tell.

Ever since I was stationed at Newhall, in each station, I had been on their pistol team. I had become pretty good with a pistol and enjoyed shooting. While at Topanga and at Malibu, I had been on the West Hollywood team and we held the championship title. For practice and to qualify, once a month we had to drive to the Sheriff's Range in East Los Angeles. That was a long ways and I felt that to get the practice needed to stay expert, we should spend more time shooting, not driving back and forth.

We got permission from the owner of some mountain property in Topanga Canyon and built a range in our own territory. It took over a month, but when we finished, we had our own pistol range. Also, for the first time in my life, I had a bad case of Poison Oak. It took another miserable month for me to get rid of it.

One day Mrs. Mason, a friend of ours, was visiting. She liked to hike, so we climbed up onto the lush green plateau that was up behind our house. When Mrs. Mason saw it, she said, "What a wonderful place for a milk cow and I know just where you can get one." I had been thinking a bit about that myself. There was no other easy way up to that plateau, except through our canyon. A cow would be safe there and that field was large enough to feed ten cows.

Later, I contacted the neighbor Mrs. Mason had told me about up in Sequit Canyon. We made a deal. I got a fine Guernsey and her calf. Borrowing a horse trailer, I set out with Katherine and Margaret Ann to get our animals. There were so many turns on that steep mountain road, I decided not to put the calf in the trailer with his mother. If the mother slipped and fell, that would be the end of him. So I tied that little fellow up and put him in the back seat of our car. That trip down the mountain was one neither Katherine nor I could ever forget. Margaret Ann got quite a kick out of it!

Bob was there when we arrived home. He helped me get those animals safely up on that plateau. That evening, Bob was given a short course on "How to milk a cow." From then on, that was his job. We all enjoyed the rich milk, the cream and the butter that were the returns from that adventure.

One day, when I was at work, a teletype message came over the line. As I read the message, I was shocked! I couldn't believe what I read, "Effective (two days later) Malibu Outpost would become a full Station. Temporary Lieutenant Nester would return to his former status of Sergeant and would turn command over to Captain Jay Morley. Sergeant Kelsey Kyle would be transferred to Malibu as an investigator!" . . . two new men to do what I had been doing for years!

To say I was shocked would be putting it mildly. I had never been called in or otherwise reprimanded for action I had taken or had failed to take. Over the years, from the start at Topanga Outpost, we had grown in personnel from four to twelve men . . . now this!

I thought I had an explanation coming . . . so I went on in to the West Hollywood station. I found that Captain Hanby had been ill and had taken sick leave. The captain relieving him was unable to give me any satisfaction, so I proceeded on downtown. I was unable to see the Sheriff, but was directed to the Undersheriff's office. He handled all criminal department matters. Remembering my last experience with the Undersheriff, I didn't have very high hopes. He hadn't changed one bit. He let me know that if it had been up to him, I never would have even been a temporary Lieutenant! It was then that I realized WHY I had never been appointed a full Lieutenant after being next up on that list for over six months. They just let that list run out and then called for another Lieutenants' examination. That took out of me any desire I had to ever take another Lieutenants' examination.

As a Sergeant, I was immediately returned to shift work at the station. If they had transferred me somewhere else, I would have felt better about it. But they didn't. After being in charge at Topanga and at Malibu for nearly five years, you can imagine just how I felt!

S.S. Coya anchored off Amapala in the Gulf of Fonseca, September, 1936.

CHAPTER 16

HONDURAS

1936

One morning, soon after all this happened, I had gone to the bank in Santa Monica on business. The manager of the bank called me, "Paul, meet an old friend of mine, John Coffee. He's a mineralogist and just retired after serving many years working for the Guggenheim's. You two should have a lot to talk about."

We did. All about mining. When we parted, I had an invitation to visit his home and meet his family.

When I told Katherine about the mining engineer, she said, "Oh, oh. There you go again." She knew only too well just what this might be leading to.

Accepting Mr. Coffee's invitation, our two families soon became friends. His life had been interesting. He had spent a good many years examining mines and prospects all over the world and his stories were fascinating! I inquired about properties he had checked and turned down. I was especially interested about those that lacked capacity (not enough proven ore) or properties that had been turned down before the cyanide or floatation systems for recovery of gold came into common usage.

One mine he told about, appealed to me. El Porventer was located in the Republic of Honduras, Central America. In 1903, that mine had run out of "high grade" free gold ore. At about the same time a series of revolutions started . . . making Honduras a dangerous place. The mine owners shut down and got out.

I encouraged JC (John Coffee) to write to Honduras and inquire about the mining in El Porventer area. Weeks later he received a reply. No foreign companies were operating in that part of Honduras.

After due consideration, JC and I decided to go to Honduras and examine that mine. If it then appeared to be worthwhile, we would attempt a lease-purchase contract on that property.

In 1936, transportation to Central America and points south was not easy. Pan American was operating, but it was the expensive way to go. The Grace Lines had equipped their coastwise freighters with passenger facilities. JC and I were able to get passage on the S.S. Coya. That ship was scheduled to carry a cargo of dynamite for the mines operating in the south. I was able to arrange a leave of absence from the Sheriff's Office.

During my absence, Katherine and Margaret Ann would go north and stay with Katherine's sister, Mrs. Margaret Arata in Portland. Bob would remain in California so that he could attend Santa Monica High School. I went north to Portland with Katherine and Margaret Ann and enjoyed a short visit there.

Returning to San Francisco, I boarded the Coya which was anchored out in the bay. They were loading dynamite from barges secured alongside. By midnight, the loading was completed and we got underway.

Several days later, we dropped anchor one mile out, off San Pedro harbor, as required by law for ships carrying dynamite. I went ashore and met Al Shaw, my brother-in-law. Al had driven out with JC and his baggage. Soon thereafter, JC and I bade Al goodbye. We took a motor boat out to the Coya and by midnight, August 22, the ship was underway.

The Coya had a full passenger list (it only carried twelve). I recall Ex-Honduran San Francisco Council, Senior Alberto Premo, his wife and son. They were returning to their home at Tegucigalpa.

Early the morning of August 28th, we arrived at Manzinallo, Mexico. Here again, because of the dynamite, we anchored over a mile off shore. All the passengers were anxious to go ashore. We didn't know that it would be our only opportunity before reaching our destination.

Manzinallo was a port that at one time harbored a fleet of fighting ships for the old Spanish Navy. It had a good sized bay with many beautiful coves. The beaches were a sun-lover's paradise and there were many local senoritas there to help decorate them.

Here, we lost one passenger and picked up another. The new passenger and I became acquainted. He spoke about as much English as I did Spanish. We paracticed a lot on each other. He told me that he had immigrated to Mexico from Poland when he was sixteen years old. After learning the language, he received his Mexican citizenship. As a fisherman, he had developed the tiburon (shark) fishing business on the west coast of Mexico. There, he owned two canneries. He recently had paid $10,000 for the shark fishing rights off the west coast of Nicaragua. Now, he was on his way there to build another cannery.

The last day or two aboard, my Polish friend tried hard to persuade me to forget the mining business and join him in the fishing/canning operation. He said he had trouble getting capable people to run his various branches. He liked Americans and he offered me a good position plus an interest in his Nicaraguan business if I would go with him. But my experience was in mining. I liked the man and even though I believed his deal was good, I turned him down. I've often wondered where I'd be today if I had accepted his offer.

During this time, JC developed a very good friendship with Sr. Premo and his family. Through the gift of gab, he acquired information about Honduras and also discovered a very close relationship between Sr. Premo and the Vice President of Honduras.

Port calls were made at Champarico and San Jose, Guatemala and at La Libertad and Acajulto, San Salvador. In each instance, the ship had to anchor out a mile or so from shore.

Finally, early in the morning of September 4th, we entered the Gulf of Fonseca and dropped anchor near Amapala, which is located on the island of Tigre. Honduras has only one western port, Amapala, in the middle of the gulf. San Francisco Bay is the only larger inland waterway on the entire Pacific Coast. San Salvador borders the Gulf to the south and Nicarauga borders it to the north. Honduras lies in between.

The Coya lost half of its passengers at Amapala. Besides JC and I, Sr. Premo and his family disembarked. It was necessary to pass through customs. I had worried some about that. When we were packing for this trip, I found out JC had a steamer trunk he was packing that had a false bottom. It was loaded with his rifle, plenty of ammunition and a large quantity of medical supplies. I had asked, "What's the reason for all the drugs?" His answer, "Don't worry about them . . . it's for the poor natives. You'll see when we get

Customs house at Amapala with the Venetian
Hotel adjoining the pier to the left.

CAMP SITE AT SANTA LUCIA

there." I wondered how and then decided, the man knew his way around and I hoped everything would be all right.

In addition to the rifle, JC had a .38 Colt Automatic and I had a .44 Smith and Wesson revolver with a good supply of ammunition. We had been advised that going to Honduras without firearms would be the silliest thing one could do. On that day, passing through customs, JC proved his ability in the use of the Spanish language. He got us through without a hitch.

We all registered at the Venetian Hotel. It was located right on the pier, over the water, in a very convenient place. It was cooler there than any other spot on that island. I never saw any more efficient toilet facilities . . . they were located where there would never be any plumbing problems.

It was a friday when we landed. We found out that we would have to stay in Amapala until monday. Weekends, the natives came to the city just like they do in all the towns and villages in Mexico and Central America. The only difference was that instead of walking, riding a donkey, mule or horse, or an oxcart, the natives around Amapala came in boats. Everything from small dugout canoes to sail and motor boats. Nobody would be leaving until sunday night or monday morning.

Very early monday morning, JC and I, with our baggage, departed for the mainland in a launch. After several hours, we came to the mouth of an estuary. Taking this narrow, but most interesting passage up through the heavy growth of the jungle to its head, we disembarked at a very small village. Aceituno was so far off the usual paths, the natives turned out in droves to see the strangers. JC and I took turns taking pictures.

By early afternoon, JC had hired two mozos (helpers) and had rented mules for us to

MOTOR BOAT WHICH BROUGHT US FROM AMAPALA TO EL ACEITUNO

ride and an oxcart to transport our supplies. Soon, we were packed, mounted and were on our way.

The road was muddy and our progress slow. It rained most all that afternoon. Workmen were cutting the jungle back from the sides of the road. I was told they had to work continuously during the rainy season to keep that jungle from taking over the road. Traveling through this kind of lowland country was a new experience for me. The tropical growth was so dense, it was impossible to see beyond a few feet from the road. Thank goodness JC had insisted we equip ourselves with very good saddle rain-slickers. It was still raining when we arrived at Goscoran that evening, but we were dry.

Goscoran was on the border between Honduras and San Salvador. Only a small river separated those two countries. It had the reputation of being kind of a tough place. JC was able to arrange for a room in the home of a school teacher who lived across the street from the town cantina. A crowd of curious natives gathered to watch as the oxcart was being unloaded. JC was intent on seeing that none of our belongings disappeared as they were being moved into our room. One overly curious drunk, who was carrying a gun on his hip, took a dislike to my partner. I was able to calm this fellow down by taking him across to the cantina and buying him a drink. Only then, I had a hard time getting rid of him. He figured it paid to be my buddy.

Later, that evening, while we were at the eating section of that cantina, this same drunk came up to JC, flipped a bandana handkerchief, which JC was wearing around his neck, up into his face. This fellow was even more drunk and was possibly dangerous. At that time JC was unarmed. So to avoid trouble, he turned and went to our quarters. Again, I was able to get

NATIVES AT EL ACEITUNO

that drunk into a better mood and he forgot all about JC.

From then on, neither one of us went anywhere without being armed. Most every man in Honduras who could afford a firearm, carried one. Those who couldn't, carried a machete, and most of the time it was in his hand.

Sept. 8- After breakfast we were on our way at 7 AM. At 11. AM we came to the Aramecina River at flood stage. I had to swim across with a line, & make fast to a tree. Upon my return across an officer Chief Inspector of the Honduranean Mounted Police Francisco Amador & a trooper rode up. Our mozos had showed their yellow when we came to this river, so Amador took things in charge. He had a fine mount & made 7 trips across the river with our lighter baggage. Then his trooper carried the three heaviest packages over hanging to our life-line with the bundles strapped to his head & up to his arm pits in water that was traveling appr. 6 miles per hour. The dist. across was approx 170 ft. A at 1.30 PM, we were all sa across with our baggage. Amador drove the oxen up. & swam them across for mozoes & incidentally he co them everything he knew To & Told them they ought be home for they were cowardly wo We arrived at Aramecina 4.00 PM in the rain. Fo lodging There with Don Calis Bda. Vanegas. We met There Senior Don Do Euseda who is Mgr. at t Powents Mine. He was leaving for Santa Lucia the mine & promised to r for us 2 days later whe the flood of the rivers subsided a bit.

228

Aramecina is a small village, just big enough to have the usual town square. A real old adobe church occupied all of one side of the square. The church was locked. I was told the priest came by every two months or so and held services for his people there. He only stayed for three days, then would be on his way to another part-time parish.

Homes, businesses and Government buildings, all constructed with adobe and tile roofs, took up two of the adjoining sides of the square. The fourth side, opposite the church, was unoccupied. In each direction, one block or so away you would be entering the jungle.

There were two small stores, a cantina and several government buildings. I was surprised to learn that village had an alcalde (mayor), a comandante (commander) and a small garrison of soldiers. There was even a telegraph office, run by the military. Honduras has a very efficient telegraph system throughout the country. Later, I was to learn they had another system of communication. If one travels through the mountains on a road or by trails, where there is no telegraph. About the time you start out, if you listen carefully, you will hear a bird call, or possibly a peculiar whistle. Listen. It will be repeated in the distance. Then listen again. If your ears are good, you might hear it again in the far distance. Nearly always, the natives know you are coming and usually know who you are and how many. It's wierd!

While JC was getting information about El Porventer and making preparations for our trip there, I practiced Spanish. It had been only a

PASSING OX CART & NATIVES IN FRONT OF DON DOMINGO'S HOUSE

few months since I first started to study. Now, if I communicated to any one other than JC, it had to be in Spanish. When it came to languages, I wasn't a fast learner. The natives for the most part, were friendly and cooperative. They payed no attention to my many mistakes.

We left Aramecina about nine o'clock in the company of Don Domingo. The Aramecina River was down to three feet and our mules crossed easily. We arrived at Santa Lucia shortly after eleven a.m. This was Don Domingo's home and we met his family. He had secured an old house for us nearby. Two native women had spent the morning cleaning, but that old house was still too dirty for us. We pitched our tent under some trees nearby and used the house for storing our supplies. Santa Lucia, was just a very small place, with several houses and not over half a dozen families.

We had no more than set up our tent, when natives commenced to stop by, asking for the help of the medico. JC would ask them what the trouble was. They would tell about their aches and pains. Usually, he would give them a pill or two for a good physic and some advise. There was never a charge made. That was something not even mentioned.

Nearly always, after a week or so, that native, or some one of his family would be back to thank JC. They would always have gifts of bananas, other tropical fruits, chickens, eggs, nearly everything. JC always gracefully accepted their gifts and everybody was happy.

That evening, JC explained to me. There were very few medical doctors in the Central Americas. Those that were there, most always, would be located in the larger cities. These poor natives couldn't go that far . . . especially when they were sick. Even if they could go, usually they didn't have the money to pay the doctor. From experience, the natives

THE ONLY BUILDING AT EL PORVENIR WHEN WE FIRST ARRIVED

had learned, most white men carried medical supplies, at least for himself. They had come to regard him as somewhat of a medico. The average white man in those countries usually had a fair knowledge of medics and how to take care of his ill's. He had helped the natives, so they came to get what help they could.

The next day, Don Domingo took us up to the mine. About fifty natives were working there. They were mining a high grade chimney, hauling ore out on their backs and generally operating under very primitive conditions. The larger pieces of ore would be crushed to a gravel size and then fed into molinetas. These, for the most part, were worked by the women. They were similar to the primitive corn grinders of the very early indians. A cup shaped hole, about twice the size of your fist, had been chiseled in solid bed rock. A small rock, just barely able to fit into this hole was used as a grinder. To make the grinding easier, a small hole was drilled into the top of the movable stone. A "Y" shaped stick was wedged into this small hole, so that one person could stand up, grasp the upper ends of the "Y" with both hands and twist it back and forth. Ore would be fed in and ground. With a small amount of water, the grinding would reduce the ore to a very fine grade. Mercury, or quick silver would be added. This quick silver would pick up the gold and form amalgum. Usually, this amalgum would come out in the form of a marble.

In order to refine the amalgum and recover the 50% plus or minus gold it contained, workers would start a fire, cut a raw potatoe in half and carve a cavity in the center just large enough for the amalgum ball to fit in. The potatoe was then wrapped in wet banana leaves and placed in the coals of the fire. After the potatoe had time to bake, it was removed from the fire and allowed to cool off. Then they

233

JOHN CHARLES, WITH THE NATIVES WHO WERE WORKING EL PORVENIR WHEN WE FIRST ARRIVED

I WAS WATCHING THE NATIVES OPERATE THEIR MOLLINETTAS

carefully opened the potatoe and removed the ball. It was very pure gold. The quick-silver had evaporated into the white of the potatoe. This is how the natives refine their gold from hard rock. JC and I took pictures of this operation.

We would have stayed at El Porventer had we been encouraged. WE WERE NOT. All those natives working there stayed under one roof. We took a picture of it!

One day at Santa Lucia, I had gone to the stream behind our camp, to get water. I heard some horsemen. Hurriedly, I filled my cans and climbed back up to our camp. Six horsemen were facing JC and he was talking to them. I put the water down, then watched and listened. JC and the one who apparently was the leader, were talking fast. I couldn't understand what they were saying. They looked like bandits to me! When JC got a chance, he said, softly, in English, "All they want is our arms and ammunition!" Then he resumed his rapid-fire Spanish. A little later he got a break and said, "If it comes to it, I'll start on the right! You take them on the left!" I wasn't surprised. They were all armed and didn't look good to me. Again JC resumed his rapid-fire Spanish. Then, all of a sudden, the commander gave an order, "Vamos!" They wheeled their horses and rapidly rode away.

JC heaved a sigh of relief, then explained: The leader of that outfit claimed to be the Comandante at Aramecina. Apparently they were on an inspection trip, which might have developed into a shakedown for us. The Comandante noticed that I carried a .44 and that I had a belt of ammunition. He told JC that he, also carried a .44 and was practically out of ammunition. JC was able to change their minds, by telling them, "We had come to Honduras at the invitation of the Vice President of their country. The Vice President knew we

236

had arms and ammunition and knew very well, we might be needing them." The Comandante swallowed that story.

Then JC went on to tell me, Honduras had passed laws prohibiting the sale or circulation of ammunition. This was meant to further help control the revolutionary condition that had existed in that country for so many years. The value of one bullet had come to be one day's work for one man. He went on to say, "This sort of a shake down, had been standard practice for comandante throughout the country. About a year or so, back when the last President of Honduras came into power, they got a good man. He started to clean up the country and was having quite a time of it.

"You know what would have happened, if we had given in to that comandante? Besides our arms and ammunition, they would have taken our belongings . . . everything they wanted. Then, when they were finished, the machete boys would come in and would clean us out of what might be left. We would have been very lucky to come out of it alive.

"Now," he said, "I've got an important, fast trip to make. I'm going up to Caridad and send a telegram to Sr. Premo. Don't think I'll be back tonight. You take care and I'll see you tomorrow." Our mozo brought up the mule JC had asked for. In short order, they were on their way. The village of Caridad was perhaps sixteen miles farther on up through the mountains to the north.

El Porventer's location was in the Department (State) of Tegucigalpa. The Department line ran through just below El Porventer. Santa Lucia and Aramecina were in the Department of Valle. For the most part, El Porventer was being controlled and operated by the lowland natives. Rivalry existed between the lowland natives and those of the high mountains.

JC and I had been busy for some days, checking El Porventer and nearby mine areas . . . taking samples, measuring and making records. My correspondence had been neglected. So I spent the balance of that day and a good part of the next, trying to catch up.

Along in the afternoon of the second day, natives started gathering. Some were ill and asked for help. Others were carrying gifts for the medico. I told them, "JC would be back shortly." They were patient . . . a lot of visiting was done while they waited.

By the time JC and the mozo arrived, a fair sized group had gathered. The gifts were presented first. In the exchange, a young rooster made his escape. He ran about 50 feet, then stopped for a moment just before entering the jungle. That moment was long enough for me. I shot his head off with my .44! You should have heard that crowd! In a low tone, in English, JC said, "Better stop there, your reputation has been established!"

It took a bit of doing for JC, even with my help, to take care of that crowd. But he made it okay. He was so tired, after he finished, he could hardly eat supper. He did, however, partake in an assortment of tropical fruits. That made him feel better.

When he finally got into the mood to talk, he told me that from Caridad he had sent a telegram to Sr. Premo. He explained what happened and asked for letters or orders of authority, from the Vice President, if possible, directed to comandantes or any other persons that might help us or hinder us. Now, all we had to do was wait and see.

The next several days, we were busy as usual, checking at the mine and surrounding areas. One day JC came up with an interesting suggestion. He asked me how much ammunition I had for my .44. I told him, "Two full boxes, besides what I had in my gun belt and in the revolver itself." Then he said, "How'd you like to take a gift of six .44 shells down to the Comandante at Aramecina?" That sounded like quite an idea to me.

Early the next morning, I was on my way to Aramecina. I wanted to check for mail and possibly there would be some word from Sr. Premo. I also felt that, with a bit of good luck, I could make a friend of the Comandante. I also had some doubts. My chief concern was that my Spanish was far from good. I thought I could fairly express myself . . . but, I wasn't sure of being able to understand everything that was said to me. Anyway, it was a chance I decided to take.

My first stop, was to see the Comandante. Thank goodness, he was there. I presented my gift and when he opened the package, he let out a yell that could be heard a block away. He was happy and grateful. One of the soldiers was called in and ordered to go out and find the fattest chicken in town. That was to be a gift for me when I was ready to return. There were letters too, from home and from Tegucigalpa. Later, I made my way back up to Santa Lucia, feeling rather proud. We had accomplished a lot that day, to establish better relations for our future.

Day by day, JC and I learned a lot more about El Porventer. The mine had been closed down for many years. Taxes had not been paid and the ownership had reverted back to the government. About a year before, natives exploring in the old mine had found a high-grade chimney. They needed dynamite, fuse, caps, carbide and all the bare necessities to operate in a crude way. Don Domingo, a former store keeper and a friend, helped solve their problem. He arranged all the necessities. In turn, they sold their gold to him, of course at quite a discount.

Don Domingo realized, operations could not go on very long that way. So he took his information about the mine and his proposition to Sr. Hector Laszio, the congressman for the Department of Valle. Sr. Laszio in turn, went to his friends, influential congressmen in the Capital, with the suggestion they form "una sociedad commercial" (a company or corporation) to denounce, and legally stake a claim on El Porventer. This was done and Don Domingo was appointed local manager with a one-eighth ownership in the sociedad. For the past year, the mine had operated under those conditions and all concerned appeared to be happy.

JC did not feel bad about this. He figured, "That high-grade chimney will last only about six months longer. All we have to do is make a good offer to the owners, then wait. When they run out of high-grade ore, they will contact us."

There was nothing more for us to do at El Porventer. We had made a good friend of Don Domingo. He couldn't read or write, but he was a very smart man. He saw the advantage of operating with modern machinery. Now, we had to convince the others. Our first stop would be Amapala, to see Sr. Hector Laszio. Then, we would go to Tegucigalpa, the capital, and contact the other owners.

We would offer to purchase El Porventer on a lease-purchase contract with no down payment. We would put into operation at the mine, a 20 ton per day capacity mill with all modern equipment. Our offer would be $90,000 for the property. Payments would be 25% of the net. After the purchase price had been paid, we would continue to pay a royalty of 12% of the net.

Our trip back to Aceituno was uneventful. We had to travel through deeper mud than when we came in. It was later in the rain season. At Aceituno, we boarded a 24 foot native bungo, a

240

large Indian canoe, hollowed out of mahogony and rigged for sailing. It was the only transportation available for our trip across the gulf to Amapala. There was a crew of three. Besides JC and I, with our baggage, there were eleven natives, three pigs and a flock of chickens, along with other produce and supplies. That boat was loaded.

In the evening, we sailed down the estuary along with the out going tide. Several hours later, just as we approached the mouth of the estuary, una tormenta, (a rain storm) struck. The sails were dropped, then the anchor. With the sail canvas, we were able to rig a cover to help keep us dry. Soon, the air under that canvas was unbearable. I felt like I was about to become asphyxiated. Every so often, to get a bit of fresh air, I would stick my head out from under the canvas. Once, just after ducking back under, something hit! A fish, about 14 inches long, slid into my lap! What a yell those natives let out! It was a needed diversion and was timed just right. I had caught a dandy without even using a hook! After several hours, the rain and wind slacked off. The anchor was hoisted and we sailed away. Just before dawn next morning, our boat tied up at the dock in Amapala.

It was sunday, October 18th. JC and I checked in at the Hotel Valencia. Glad to be back in civilization again, we cleaned up and had a good breakfast. Then we contacted Sr. Hector Laszio. He was only able to see us for a short time, as he was leaving for Tegucigalpa on the 10:30 a.m. boat. Later that day, we did see Sr. Manuel Beoletto, another one of the El Porventer owners. Sr. Laszio had contacted him and suggested he come to see us. We visited for several hours. After he left, both JC and I thought we had gained another friend. Our hopes for the future took another jump.

That afternoon, the S.S. Coya stopped by

on her way north. We shipped a box containing clothes and equipment we could not very well take aboard a plane. Also mineral samples which we wanted to assay in the United States.

Tuesday, we crossed over to the mainland by launch and disembarked at San Lorenzo. There, JC was able to discourage the Customs officers from checking over our baggage. By two o'clock that afternoon, we were aboard a Ford Bus, heading for Tegucigalpa. The first two hours, we traveled on a fairly good gravel road, through jungle country and passed several small farms along the way. Vegetation was most all tropical at first, then as we gained altitude, we entered the pine forests and the scenery became more beautiful. In the high mountains, we came into country very much like that of the Oregon Coastal Range. Vegetation was similar. Evergreen blackberries were plentiful. I was told, the altitude was 5500 feet at the summit.

Just about dark, we stopped at a roadside inn for supper. The food was good, or we were exceptionally hungry. It was raining when we left there and continued until we arrived at Tegucigalpa about nine o'clock. We registered at the Palace Hotel, which faced the city plaza. Tired, we both "hit the hay."

Next morning, Sr. Hector Laszio was contacted. He helped us set up a meeting with the other owners of El Porventer. At that meeting JC presented our plan. After some discussion, it was suggested to us that it would be better for all concerned to present the El Porventer owners with a written offer in Spanish, for their future study.

Sr. Premo was contacted. After a nice visit with that gentleman and his family, he was told of our progress. Sr. Premo offered to help us in the preparation of this paper. We purchased a Civil and a Mining Code and the three of us went to work. In a reasonable time the job was finished. The owners of El Porventer were presented with our "Offer in the Spanish Language."

That was all we could do for now . . . it was time to leave. In order to get legal clearance from the country, we had to make the rounds of the Minister of War, the Chief of Police, the Honduras Bureau of Investigation and the office of Internal Affairs, to get our passports stamped. Then, there was the matter of getting back a $100 deposit fee each of us had to put up when we entered the country. That took some time.

After saying adios to all our friends, by 2:30 that afternoon, we were on our way north, aboard a DC-3 Pan American airliner.

We had a pleasant trip back to the States. Stopping overnight at Guatemala City, we had time to see that beautiful City. Upon Arrival at Mexico City, we stayed for several days.

JC had worked in the silver mines at Pachuca, Mexico, for a number of years. We made a trip out there and he was able to meet and visit with some of his old friends. The Pachuca mining area holds the record. It has been producing silver continuously for over 400 years and was still taking out ore at the rate of 5000 tons per day.

Late the afternoon of October 28, 1936, JC and I arrived back in Los Angeles. A few days later I was in Portland. After a short visit, Katherine, Margaret Ann and I were back home in our cabin near the beach north of Santa Monica.

Now, all we had to do with regards to El Porventer, was wait.

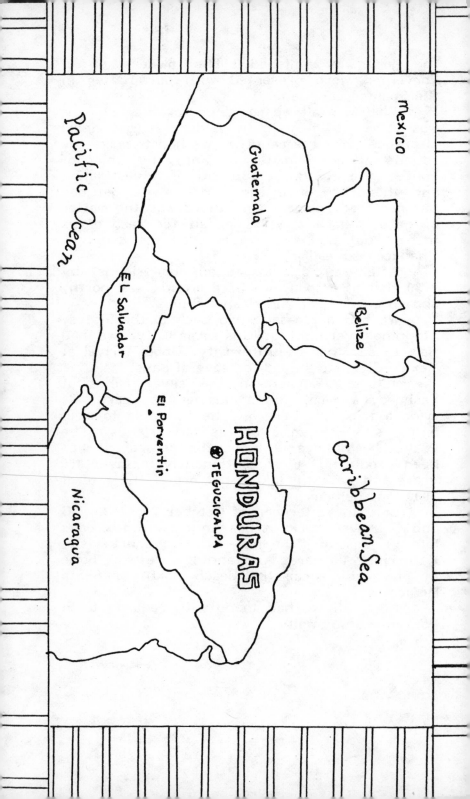

CHAPTER 17

SOUTHERN CALIFORNIA'S

FIRES AND FLOODS

1937 - 1938

Upon my return, I was put back to work as a desk sergeant at Malibu. It was mighty good to be back home and living with my family again. Most of our spare time, Katherine, Margaret Ann and I spent on the beach. We went in the ocean swimming most every day.

One day, along about the middle of March, 1937, JC called me on the phone, "I finally got the letter we've been waiting for. Guess they've run out of the high grade in the Domingo Stope. They want to do business with us."

In a few days, JC was on his way south on a Pan American Airliner.

March 27, 1937, I received a telegram from him: "Purchase Option signed with Porventer owners." This was my "Get Busy Signal."

I shipped the baggage JC had packed before he left. Then, I purchased and shipped a small pilot mill and the accessory machinery we had picked out. This mill, when set up at El Porventer, would make it possible to test-run ore from the mine and would give us the information we needed to select the proper refining equipment.

Some time later, I took a trip up into the

desert, north of Mojave, to look over some used milling machinery. The mine there had closed down and the owner was trying to sell the machinery. He picked me up and took me some distance beyond Mojave. Just after we left the main highway, it started to rain. By the time we arrived at the mine, the rain had turned into a full fledged storm.

By the time I finished checking over the machinery, it was late and we decided it would be safer and better to stay overnight right there. That storm continued all through the night. The next day, it took all the daylight hours just to get back to the main highway. At the first opportunity, I tried to call home, but the wires were down and I couldn't get through. When we arrived in Santa Monica, the Pacific Coast Highway was closed. Bad mud slides had the road blocked between Santa Monica Canyon and Malibu. Again, I tried to call home, but the phone was still out. I was able, however, to contact my sister, Monica, who lived in Los Angeles. She informed me that Katherine, Margaret Ann and Bob were okay and were safe at home there with them. They had been worried about me. The owner of that mine machinery proved to be a good friend. He drove me all the way out to south Los Angeles to the home of Monica and Al.

This is what happened to my family after I left for the desert: It started to rain and that rain got steadily heavier through the day. After dark, that evening, there was a crash, out in back, behind the house. Katherine and Bob took a flashlight and went to see what happened. I had rigged a sort of "V" shaped bulkhead to guide the water coming down the ravine into a three foot square flume which ran under our garage and out to a gutter on the highway. That bulkhead had collapsed and part of our back porch had been carried away. With all the water coming down out of that canyon, it gave them a scare. They checked to see about getting the car out. The garage was flooded with mud and refuse and they both felt the car probably wouldn't run even if they could have gotten it out.

Back in the house, Katherine telephoned Monica and Al. Al told her to "stay put." He would come and get them. Soon after making that telephone call, the phone went bad and the lights went out! What a night they must have had!

Al called the Highway Patrol and was informed that mud slides and very dangerous road conditions made it impossible for anyone to travel north of Santa Monica on the coast road. It was a good thing he had been to our home many times and was able to figure another way to get there.

Starting out at daylight the next morning, Al went out Sunset Boulevard, through Pacific Palisades, then down the grade to a point one half mile from the Coast Highway. There, the roadway was a mill-race. He stopped, turned the car around and parked above in a safe spot. Sunset was full of water curb to curb and that water was traveling fast. He waded across and hiked up the canyon on the west side. Climbing through the brush up the hill to the back of the Castellemar sub-division, he made his way west. Crossing the Parker Canyon, he again climbed up onto the plateau that was above and back of our cabin. From there, he made his way down the canyon to his destination.

How happy Katherine, Margaret Ann and Bob must have been when Al arrived. It didn't take them long to get ready and head out of there. Al took the lead, retracing his way back to his car. Crossing Sunset Boulevard with that fast running water was quite an experience. Margaret Ann had the best of it. She rode across on Al's shoulders. They were mighty

Katherine, Margaret Ann and I with Mitzi.

Margaret Ann on our front porch.

happy when they arrived at Monica and Al's. To be safe, in a nice warm comfortable home after an experience like theirs was sincerely appreciated. That storm had not bothered people in the south part of Los Angeles.

It was several days before workmen got the road open for one-way traffic on the coast. They had to bulldoze a trench through the mud, wide enough for passage. That trench ran for miles. On our way home, we passed the Sunset Intersection. The Standard Oil service station there was filled with mud five to six feet deep.

Our place was a mess. The car had to be dug out. Then, it wouldn't run. I finally concluded, it was best to turn it in on a brand new Ford. Getting that place back in shape took quite a while. We felt good when that mess was finally cleaned up.

Late in the spring of 1938, JC returned to the United States, with the results he had gathered from operating our small mill. We were coming along about on schedule. We were also about broke. Our operations, getting that small mill up to the mine and going had cost plenty. What we needed next, was proper financing.

On July 8, 1938, at Reno, Nevada, El Porventer Mining Company of Honduras, was incorporated under the laws of the State of Nevada. In exchange for the work we had done so far, together with the contract rights, JC and I, along with a few friends and relatives who had assisted us in this enterprise, received one third of the stock of the corporation. This stock would be held in escrow for us. The balance of the stock would be sold to raise the finances necessary to comply with the contract and get El Porventer operating as it should.

There were many things to be done down south. JC chose to return there. He was better qualified for that work and he wanted no part of the job left to be done here.

I realized, with a shock, that incorporating that company was only the first step. Many other things had to be done. It was necessary to write up and publish a "Prospectus" before any stock could be sold. The one finally completed was eleven pages of single-spaced, typewritten information on El Porventer and it had to be correct.

After that, came the job of selling the stock. Did you ever try to sell anything that was actually a speculation and located in a foreign country with a reputation like Honduras? IT WASN'T EASY!

For some time I had been working the midnight to eight a.m. shift at Malibu. That way, I could do what I had to do in the day time. For months, I had worked very hard . . . and it paid off. Funds started coming in. Each time a ship left for the small ports of Central America, we made a shipment. Mine supplies, mill machinery, cyanide tanks, floatation cells and just about everything. Finally, I thought, El Porventer was going along okay.

One saturday, I decided, I had earned a day off . . . a day of rest at home. The next day, November 25, 1938, was Margaret Ann's fourth birthday. Katherine had planned a party for her. A group of children about her age had been invited. We were preparing for this party and had just finished lunch.

The phone rang and I answered. It was my friend Bob Fox, a sergeant at Malibu Station. Bob said, "Paul, I thought you should know. A bad fire started in the Fernwood District less than an hour ago. It's traveling your way and it's already about half way there!"

I thanked him for the information. I went out on the porch and looked back up the hill. The sky was black with smoke clouds! I ran to the water hose and tried to turn on the water.

Not a drop came! There were too many other houses lower than ours and their owners had spotted the fire and were wetting down.

Quickly, I got the car out of the garage and headed it towards Santa Monica. We started loading our possessions. Before the car was full, heavy black smoke was burning our eyes. Katherine and Margaret Ann got in and I suggested they drive to the Kohlers, friends of ours who lived in the Pacific Palisades. Margaret Ann kept calling for Mitzi, our pet chow. She had three very young puppies. I made a run up back of the house, picked up the box those puppies were in and brought it to the car. Mitzi was right on my heels. We made room for them and Katherine took off for the Pacific Palisades.

Bob had been helping with the loading. Now, he helped me disconnect a brand new Electrolux refrigerator we had in the kitchen and we were able to get it out and tumble it over an ice-plant covered slope that went down to the road.

The heavy black smoke got so bad, we could hardly see. It became dangerous to go up on the main floor level. So we started working from the basement and garage. We got my tools and quite a supply of fruit which had been stored in lug boxes. Several piles of our belongings were placed on the edge of the road.

Conditions finally became unbearable. Our eyes were burning so bad, we could hardly see. We made our way across the road and down to the ocean. Wading out into the water, we put our heads down to within a foot or two of the water. There, we could see and we could breath fresh air. Some distance away, looking under that smoke, we could see possibly a dozen others. They were doing just what we were doing . . . trying to breath fresh air and hoping to see.

In about ten or fifteen minutes and it felt like an hour, that cloud of black smoke rolled off to the east. Now, we could see and our house was in 100% blaze! The hills on each side of it looked like flaming arms as the brush burned away! After a while, when the intense heat subsided a bit, we climbed back up onto the road. There were three piles of smouldering ashes where we had left our belongings. One pile consisted of broken fruit jars and the mess of their spilled contents. I found a few jars which had not burst, but the rubbers had melted. Most of my tools were okay. Then we spotted the refrigerator in a bed of ice-plant. It was hot, but okay. Our house was just a pile of smouldering ashes! All we saved from it, were my tools, the refrigerator and just what we had been able to put in the car. It all happened so fast, we hardly had time to feel bad. We were just thankful no one was hurt. Before that fire was stopped, it had consumed over 200 homes between Malibu and the Sepulvida Pass Freeway!

For six years, we had been fully covered with fire insurance. Then, about a month before the fire, when our last term came to an end, the insurance company notified us they were no longer insuring properties in that area. I had tried hard to obtain coverage, but had not been successful. Then, just a few days before the fire, I had asked an old time insurance man I knew, John Wall, if he could help me. When I told him my story, he said he would see. That was all.

Several days after the fire, just on a hunch, I called him on the phone . . . told him who was calling and he interrupted: "Thank you Paul for that check . . . you know, that check dated November 20, 1938, made out to the Right Insurance Company for a $45 dollar premium due for the fire insurance on that house of yours. Thank you Paul for getting it to me so promptly . . . that was so important. Sorry you lost your home."

I THANKED him. Then, as soon as I could, I made out the check and delivered it to his home personally. Within ten days, I received from the insurance company a check for $1200 which was the maximum allowed for small houses in that area. THANK GOD FOR SOME PEOPLE.

We were able to rent a partially furnished cabin on the beach near Los Flores. It took the best part of a week to find this cabin and to get moved in. The Kohlers had proven to be true friends. They had gone all out to care for us and make their home ours. Thanks to them and to our many friends and relatives, we were able to get a start with clothing, bedding, kitchen utensils, dishes and the many other necessary items.

That winter, we went through another harrowing experience. At the time of the month when we were having the highest and lowest tides, a bad storm hit the coast. At each high tide during that storm, our beach cabin was in danger of being knocked down and washed away. Several other cabins had already been lost in this manner. We kept our car packed with the few remaining valuable properties we possessed. Again, the good Lord must have been watching over and caring for us. We made it through okay.

Katherine had been spending considerable time in Santa Monica looking for a suitable home. Finally, she found just what she was looking for. A nice house on 18th Street, in the first block north of Montana. We used the balance of our insurance money to make a down payment and moved in. That was just in time. Nomber 22, 1939, Katherine Elizabeth, our second daughter was born. It was great to have another girl at our home.

oNewhall

VENTURA CO.
LOS ANGELES CO.

WEST
LOS ANGELES COUNTY

San Fernando Valley

Camp
#8

oWest Hollywood

TO

Malibu
o

Topanga
Outpost
o

CITY OF LOS ANGE

Santa Monica

□ BURDETTE
AIRPORT

*Santa Monica
Bay*

Palos Verdes

LO
BE

San Pedro

Pacific Ocean

CHAPTER 18

ROAD CAMP #8

1939 - 1940

One morning, when I was working the day shift at Malibu, an order came in over the teletype. "Attention Sergeant Nester, Effective Saturday (the next day), at 6 a.m., you will report to the Sergeant Ray Ross, officer in charge of Road Camp #8. Sergeant Ross will spend the day instructing you in the proper operation of a road camp. Upon his departure that evening, the responsibility for operation of that camp will be turned over to you. (Signed) Undersheriff."

This was a surprise for me. Never had I worked at such a place and I didn't expect to be sent to a road camp. I knew nothing about such things. I did know that Camp #8 was located in the Santa Monica mountains and that it was the only "loser camp" (a "loser" is a felony prisoner who has already served a term for a former crime) operated by Los Angeles County.

How Katherine would take this, I had no way of knowing. Working at a road camp was a full time job, with only three days off every two weeks. Not much of a break for a married man, just when we were nicely settled in our new Santa Monica home. Katherine and Margaret Ann liked it there. Possibly, when I was in charge, I could get home more often. Being transferred without ever having been asked, meant one thing to me . . . I had no choice.

The next morning, I drove up in the mountains to my destination. It was located in Los Virgenes Canyon on a road that was being built over to Malibu Lake. Later, it would become part of Mulholland Drive. A group of buildings on the road high up gave a splendid view of the valley. They formed a semi-circle in a grove of old oak trees. The location would have made a great vacation camp site.

There were three old barracks buildings with a capacity for twenty men each. Then, a cook house and dining room, a main office with captain's quarters, an engineer's office and quarters, a building for county employees, a store room, shops and other out buildings.

Sergeant Ross and I had met before. He appeared happy to greet me. I arrived just in time for breakfast. The bell rang and from all over the camp, people made their way to the dining hall. Officers took their seats at a special table. The prisoners lined up out in front and waited for the second bell. On that signal, they filed in and took their seats at regular assigned places, six tables with ten men to a table. No talking was allowed for the prisoners, in the dining room, until the camp captain (Sergeant Ross) entered the dining room and walked from one end to the other. Silently he made a count to see that each table was full. No one missing. Then with a nod of his head, or a wave of his hand, he gave the order to proceed . . . eat. Immediately, normal talking was resumed. Waiters were prisoners assigned to the cook. Our breakfast was nothing to boast about . . . satisfactory. As each person finished his meal, he got up and left the room.

At the officers' table, I was introduced to the few men that were there on duty that day. Since it was a weekend, just a skeleton crew was left to run the camp.

After breakfast, Sergeant Ross started showing me and telling me what my duties would be. Saturday was always a cleanup day. Everybody worked. All bunks, lockers and everything loose was carried outside, so the barracks could be scrubbed, then hosed down. All blankets were cleaned, shaken, then aired out. This shaking was done by count in a military manner. You sure could hear those blankets snap.

Usually by noon, the barracks would be dry and everything was moved back inside. In the afternoon, the inmates could do anything as long as they obeyed the rules and regulations. Most of the fellows used this time to take care of personal laundry, to write letters, or just to read and rest.

All prisoners in Camp #8 were felons. Not just once, but each man had already served a term in some other prison or penitentiary. They had been in trouble before, had been apprehended, convicted and served their time. Now, they were back again, serving a second time for another offense. This time, each man had applied for probation. After an investigation and the recommendation of probation officers, the judge had seen fit to give them another chance. First however, he had sentenced each one to prison for the time prescribed by law for their latest offense. Then, as a part of probation, he had set that sentence aside and required that they serve six, nine or twelve months in a county road camp.

Los Angeles County Sheriff's Department operated eight camps at that time building roads through the mountains. This gives felony prisoners a job to do. The Captain of Camp #8 was actually a Sheriff's sergeant, but at camp, he was called 'Captain.' He was responsible for the prisoners, their discipline and for the operation of the camp. To supervise road construction, there was a County Road Department Engineer. Three regular deputy sheriffs who were qualified as road foremen bossed the crews. There was a bulldozer operator, a power shovel operator, a powder man and two truck drivers . . . all county employees. Then there was a chef, most important of all. Eleven free men operated that camp.

An honor system prevailed. Nobody was ever locked up. At no time were any fire-arms in sight. Strict military discipline and the enforcement of rules and regulations made operations possible. When a new man arrived, he was told to study the rules and regulations which were posted on a bulletin board. If he didn't understand them, he was told to ask for an explanation. They were divided into felonies and misdemeanors for camp purposes only. The felonies were serious and for their violation a prisoner could have his probation revoked and he would be on his way to San Quentin very fast. An example of a felony would be violation of the camp limits, an imaginary line approximately 100 yards out away from any camp building. . . For a misdemeanor, a petty violation, a man could lose his visiting privileges or spend a saturday afternoon chopping wood. Winters were cold and we used a lot of wood.

The main office was headquarters. It took up half the space of a small cabin. The other half was sleeping quarters for the captain and his assistant. The office also served as a sick-bay, a store-room and a general hang-out for the camp's officers.

Every weekday for about a half hour

after supper, the store would be open. Each prisoner earned fifty cents a day for his work and most of that was spent for cigarettes, candy, toothpaste and a few other odds and ends. Operating the store was just another one of the captain's chores. A line would form outside an office window. It was a nuisance for the captain, but mighty important for each of the prisoners.

Time had gone by so fast that day. So many things had been told and shown to me, I felt like I was in a whirl. It was after ten o'clock that evening when Sergeant Ross extended his hand to bid me farewell. He said, "Paul, I wish you good luck . . . for me, I am happy. . . I have just completed the last day of the most miserable year of my life! . . . Goodbye."

But I wouldn't let go of that hand. I wanted to know, WHY? Perhaps, I might be able to do something about it. . . Ray finally sat down and started talking.

He said that when he was transferred there, he had been promised that his stay at Camp #8 would be for only one year. Now, his superiors were keeping their promise. . . For years, that camp had the reputation of being a miserable place. . . He went on saying, "Trouble will start, but no matter what happens, don't get too excited about it. Take it easy and search out 'WHY.' Most of the time you will trace it down to your roommate, the man who is in command when you are away. . . Don't underestimate him. He is well educated and smooth. . . . He does things that cause other people misery. . . Be careful. . . Don't ever make a move against him unless you have good proof in writing with witnesses. That man has powerful friends."

When I asked what he does, I was told, "Most everything. But I'm not going to get into that. . . To prove my point, just check into what that fellow's past has been. That will give you the story. . . You will probably be his main target for awhile, so 'Watch Out.'"

Ray finally left. Don't know . . . but I didn't sleep very well that night!

The next day, Sunday, the church people started arriving about ten o'clock in the morning to hold services. Various religions were represented and each group had some support. The services were all held in the park-like visiting area. It was ideal for something like this.

Along about one o'clock in the afternoon, prisoner's visitors started arriving. Visitors were allowed on Sundays between one and five. Quite often, their families or friends would bring well filled picnic baskets. This was encouraged as long as the rules and regulations were followed by the visitors as well as by the inmates. All the visitors were gone by five thirty.

The remainder of that day I spent getting better acquainted with Bill Hoeff, the deputy who was on duty with me over the week end. Bill was perhaps ten years older than I. He was a road crew foreman and an expert stone mason. His crew constructed the rock culverts, bridges and all the other stonework along the road. He was friendly . . . he told me and showed me a lot that helped.

Monday morning, from six on, the county employees that had been away over the weekend started returning. Breakfast was at seven and most all the workmen were there by that time. I met the engineer, the two other deputies that were road foremen, the machine operators and the powder man.

Bill Hoeff had told me about the formalities at the start of each work day. He offered to show me, by doing what my job would be, for the first time.

At 7:55 a.m., he took a whistle from a

hook in the office and gave three sharp blasts on that whistle. That was the signal for all the road working prisoners to fall-in. They formed a double line on the road directly in front of the office. Then Bill read the orders of the day. Finishing that, he blew the whistle again and those men broke ranks and scrambled to the trucks that were waiting for them. When each foreman was satisfied he had his full crew, the trucks pulled out heading for the work areas.

By a quarter past eight, the camp was nearly empty. The only ones remaining were an orderly who was a general helper about camp, the camp mechanic and those assigned to the cook for kitchen help.

I used a good portion of the morning getting acquainted with the chef and learning how that important part of the system worked. The chef explained about supplies. They were ordered through the Engineer's Department. He said that twice a week, he would submit a list of needed supplies to the engineer. Each tuesday and friday, the 'Fish Truck' ('Fish' is a nick-name for a new prisoner), would bring in these items along with the mail and any new prisoners for the camp.

When I asked about the cooks, he told me there was always a surplus of good cooks that were prisoners. He went on to tell me there were always a number of prisoners who wanted to work as waiters or kitchen help. When he needed a man, he would go to the captain and ask for help. It was up to the captain to make an appointment. As time went by, I found that this was the custom not only with kitchen help but with every other appointment. The captain did have authority.

At lunch that day, I had my first good opportunity to size up my assistant. He was a man, perhaps ten years older that I, about my height, but weighing 200 pounds or more. That man kept the conversation rolling all through the meal. The engineer and all the others were congenial and friendly. I believed I could like them all.

That first week went by fast. I even started to become a bit friendly with my assistant. Then friday night came and I went on my first days off. Every other week I got three days off in a row, saturday, sunday and monday.

I was happy to be back home again after eleven days away. Katherine and Margaret Ann and the baby made it okay all by themselves. The only trouble was, my visit home was so short, the time passed so fast. Before I knew it, it was tuesday morning just before eight o'clock and I was back in the mountains driving into the camp.

There was something strange about the appearance of the visiting area. All the tables and benches had been moved up on that barren hillside between the prisoners' and the visitors' outhouses. Nothing but a cleared area remained where the visiting grounds had been.

A group of officers, including the engineer and my assistant were standing out in front of the office talking. I approached the group. Looking directly at my assistant, I asked, "What happened to the visiting area?"

He answered, "Oh, I thought I would put in a flower garden in its place. Up on the hill is a good enough place for the visiting . . . In the sun, the visitors won't stay so long!"

I was furious and told him, "Get your crew and put those tables and benches right back where they were! . . . and don't you ever move anything else around this camp without asking me about it first! . . . Get that done before you take your crew out on the road this morning!

It was 7:55 and I blew the whistle. When the prisoners were all lined up and counted off, it was blown again and they loaded up and were on their way, that is, . . . all but my assistant and his crew. They went to work moving park tables and benches.

For the next week or so, things seemed to go along fairly well without anything serious happening. Then, on monday, at noon, when the dinner bell rang and the dining hall filled, I walked down the center isle to make my count. I raised my hand as a signal for them to start to eat. . . Apparently, that was their signal too. Every prisoner in that dining room got up from their tables and walked out!

Following them out, I called to one of the corporals (a prisoner who has been appointed by the captain and had been placed in charge of his barracks. He ran things there and was a great help to the officers of the camp), "Get the other corporals and come down to the office." I went to the office and waited. I knew there was trouble brewing, but what kind, I didn't know.

In a few minutes, the three corporals showed up. I asked, "What's the beef?" and waited.

One of the corporals spoke up. "Captain, you're new here. We thought maybe you could help us. Haven't you noticed how cruddy our meals are? We work hard and feel that we have more coming to us than the lousy chow they've been feeding us. This is our way of asking for your help."

I had noticed the considerable difference between what the officers were receiving and what the prisoners got. I thought they were entitled to better food and answered, "Don't know whether I can help you or not. But if you'll give me a bit of time, I'll give it a try. Now, what are you going to do about this STRIKE?"

Their spokesman said, "Blow the whistle at one o'clock and see."

I blew the whistle at the usual time and every man went to his truck as if nothing had happened. They worked all that afternoon without lunch and there was no complaining.

The next morning, I left camp and made a trip downtown. I went to the County Jail and had a talk with the Jail Steward. From there, I paid a visit to the Supply Division of the County Road Department. I got a considerable amount of information.

By the time I returned, I knew I operated a camp that had established a record for economy in competition with the seven other camps operating in Los Angeles County. Our cost per meal was nine and a fraction cents per prisoner. The average cost at all camps was twelve and a half cents for a meal. The allowance set by the county was fifteen cents per meal. This, I had been told, gave great credit to the engineer and the chef at Camp #8.

It didn't take me long after that to change the kind of meals we got. That, made the prisoners happy . . . but, it also made an engineer very mad at me . . . some of the supervisors weren't too pleased about it either.

When the weather started to get hot, I formed the habit of taking a walk each night after the ten o'clock count and the lights had been turned out. Moonlight nights were special. . . I had brought Mitzie (our chow) from home with me and she enjoyed the walks as much as I did. We would follow the road a mile or so to its end, then return. One evening, we were on our return and had just rounded a curve, when we met three prisoners who were walking towards us. When they saw us, they ran and tried to hide in the brush alongside the road. I sent Mitzi with orders to "fetch."

When they were all back on the road and I felt sure of their identity, I said, "What a beautiful night it is for walking." I knew that this was their only reason for being where they

BRIGHT
F. CRIMINAL DIVISION

NUREMBERG
F. RECORDS AND IDENTIFICATION

ARTHUR C. JEWELL
UNDER-SHERIFF

WALTER D. GILMAN
CHIEF, CIVIL DIVISION

CLEM PEOPLES
CHIEF, JAIL DIVISION

COUNTY OF LOS ANGELES

OFFICE OF THE SHERIFF

EUGENE W. BISCAILUZ, SHERIFF

LOS ANGELES, CALIFORNIA

February 2, 1940.

SERGEANT PAUL NESTOR,
Road Camp #8,
Office.

My dear Sergeant Nestor:

It is indeed with a great deal of pleasure that I
am addressing this letter to you, endorsing the commendation
of Chief Peoples, Jail Division, for the work you have done
as Sergeant in charge of Road Camp No.8.

I wish to assure you that it is the splendid
cooperation of the executives such as yourself that brings
the Sheriff's Office to the favorable attention of the citizens
of this County, and you are doing your bit to help in main-
taining this fine reputation.

Sincerely yours,

E. W. BISCAILUZ, SHERIFF

ACJ:E
CC-Chief Peoples

A. C. JEWELL, Undersheriff

were. In the direction they were heading, there was nothing but mountains and they knew it. They were just doing what I was doing. Then I said, "Don't go too far. I haven't seen anybody." Mitzi and I resumed our trip back to the camp.

From that time on, very late at night, when I was alone, I commenced to receive messages. A knock on the outside of the cabin, along with Mitzi's groul, would wake me up . . . then a low voice from out in the darkness would give me a message. Such as, "Some dope or liquor is being delivered at a certain time and place," or some other important message.

I would thank them. This put me in a position to do something about it. On several occasions when I received information of this kind, the culprits would be caught, handcuffed to a pole or tree along the road and word would be sent to the Sheriff's Station to have a patrol pick them up. It wasn't long before they would be serving their time in San Quentin. After that sort of an occurrence, at the breakfast count, I would pay no attention to the vacant place or places. After breakfast, however, there would be a rush to the bulletin board. There, they would read:

> (Time and Date)
> (Name) apprehended in violation of Rule #
> Now in the County Jail awaiting trans-
> portation to San Quentin.

This didn't happen very often with me. But with my assistant, I wasn't at the camp long before I became aware of a habit he had (and this happened always on my days off) of sending prisoners into the County Jail with recommendation that their probation be revoked for cause: "Failure to obey the rules and regulations of the camp." I didn't like it. I felt he shouldn't have the authority.

Once, over a holiday, I had the time off and had made arrangements to take Katherine and Margaret Ann on a trip with me. One of the trustees had been especially friendly with Mitzie and had offered to take care of her during my absence. When I returned, Mitzie was gone! I never saw her again!

A few days later, another mysterious knock woke me up about three a.m. The voice said, "Your assistant left camp at 4 a.m. (the date of the holiday) with Mitzie. He returned at 5 o'clock without her.

I thanked him. The next day, I made a trip down to the nearest dog pound. There, I picked up a friendly police dog. I returned to the camp just as the afternoon line-up was forming. Walking with the dog up to the group of officers, the engineer made the remark, "That don't look like Mitzie."

Looking my assistant straight in the eyes, I said, "No, but I'm going to give the son-of-a-bitch that got Mitzie a chance to get this dog too . . . and when he does, I'm going to get him!" That man's eyes gave him away.

The next weekend, I was off. Before leaving camp, I sought out one of the corporals who I knew and trusted and who didn't like my assistant or his ways. I asked if it was possible to keep a secret watch at night of the possible goings and comings of my assistant. He volunteered for the job. My assistant would be watched and a record made of his actions. In case he left camp, I wanted several witnesses including at least one officer.

When I returned to camp the following tuesday, the police dog was gone. Later, that same morning, my friend, the corporal slipped me a paper. It was a complete report with listed witnesses and signatures, including one of the officers. My assistant had left camp with the police dog at four o'clock monday morning. There was an assembly of witnesses waiting for

267

him when he returned without the dog at 5:30 a.m.

Now, I thought I had enough on my assistant to get rid of him. An officer in charge at the camp, leaving without notifying another officer to take charge, violates Officers' Regulations. It's serious.

Next day, I went downtown to see the Chief Jailor. I told him why I had come in and laid my report on his desk. He read it and laughed. Then he said, "Paul, you're the first officer from that camp who didn't come in the first month he had charge, wanting to get rid of that man. You are also the first one to bring in writing a list of complaints against him. I think with this, it might be possible to get rid of that fellow. However, he's a personal friend of the Undersheriff. I'll set up an appointment with the boss and you'll hear from me in a day or two. Even with this, I don't know. But we'll do the best we can."

That bothered me. What if, even with all this evidence, nothing would be done? Thinking about that made me mad! I took the elevator down. As I got off, you know who was waiting for that elevator?! Yes, it was the Undersheriff!

Like the politician that he was, he said, "Paul. Glad to see you. How have you been? How's things out at the camp?"

He caught me just at the wrong time and I answered without thinking, "Damn rotten! . . . and if you don't transfer that _____ _____ friend of yours out pretty soon, you just might be sending out your homicide squad! The Jailor has my report with all the details."

The Undersheriff said, "Now, Paul. Calm down. Go on back to camp and things will work out."

About three hours later, when I arrived at the camp, my assistant had already departed. He had received orders from the Undersheriff to pack up and get out immediately! He obeyed and I never saw him again.

It didn't take long after that, for Camp #8 to get the reputation of being a good place to work and the best place to eat (if you were doing time) in Los Angeles County.

PLANE ARRIVES AT ARMECINA

CHAPTER 19

BACK TO HONDURAS

1940 - 1941

For some time, I had been a very busy man. For El Porventer, I had kept the finances coming in, purchased the machinery, equipment and supplies needed and had seen to it that the mine proceeded as it should.

My brother-in-law, Al Shaw assisted me in everything he could. He, like I, was working full time on his regular job as well. Al took care of the shipping. Unless one has had experience coping with the U.S. Customs rules and regulations, it's hard to visualize how complicated that can be.

How Katherine was able to take all of this, I will never know. But she had faith and all of us hoped and prayed that this very difficult period would not last long.

Fortunately, long ago, JC had put me in touch with an engineer. Jack Donivan was an expert in the operations of a mine milling plant. With his help, I had been able to make a good selection of machinery. After accomplishing that, when Donivan got word our mill was up the mountain and nearing completion, he quit

CATHEDRIAL AT TEGUCIGALPA

HOTEL AT TEGUCIGALPA

his job at a mine near Mojave and went to Honduras. He was working for us, there, now.

JC for a long time had been just as busy in Honduras as I had been in California. All machinery and supplies arriving at Amapala had to be trans-shipped to Aceituno. From there, it was hauled to the mine by oxcart.

At the mine, lumber and timbers had to be made from logs taken from nearby forests and milled in the most primitive way. Then building of a mill, shops, a cook house along with engineer's and foreman's quarters. Then the mine itself needed cleaning up. Re-timbering in many places was necessary. Yes, JC had been busy.

Shortly before Christmas, 1940, I received word JC was on his way back to the States. This was good, he deserved a break. When I went to the airport to pick him up, and saw him, I was shocked! I took him home. His wife took one look and called the doctor. The doctor sent him to the hospital.

What a change. JC was about 70 years old and looked 80. When I first met him, he looked and acted younger than 60. Working too long under difficult conditions had taken its toll. The doctors advised rest and lots of it. A month later, they said, he never should return to Honduras. From that time on, I knew I would have to take his place. There was no other way. Al would have to take care of things here.

One of our largest shipments ever, was made ready and sent to the docks at San Pedro. It included an assayers furnace and everything an assayer would need. We had shipped one before, but somehow it got lost in the shipping. We also ordered from San Francisco, such things as dynamite, fuse, caps, carbide, cyanide and floatation reagents.

Once again, I went downtown to see the Undersheriff. When I asked for a leave of absence, I was promptly turned down. He told me if I wanted to go to Honduras, I would have to quit. I didn't give him the satisfaction of an answer. Returning to camp, I very carefully went over everything with my assistant, Bill Hoeff. Then I wished him well and departed.

At 3:45 a.m., January 28, 1941, I was aboard a Mexican Airliner that took off from Grand Central Airport in Burbank, on its way to Mexico City. Flying over Los Angeles in the darkness of early morning, seeing the lights of that big city is always quite an experience. We followed the coast south easterly until we were about to approach San Diego, then headed inland. The plane landed at Mexicali, Mexico, and the passengers all went through customs.

I got the blues as that plane made its way south over the monotonous Mexican Desert. Leaving my family hadn't been easy. Could it have been that now I was leaving not only my wife and daughter, but two daughters? Then, another thing was bothering me. Would I be able to do the job, knowing no more than I did about the Spanish language? Why hadn't I studied harder?

About the time we got to Manzinello, the plane encountered strong head winds and stormy rain squalls. We arrived at Guadalajara late and were compelled to stay overnight there. Mexican law at the time, forbade flying after sunset. Next morning, we got an early start and arrived in Mexico City in time to catch the Pan American Airliner that came through from Brownsville, Texas. That plane put us in Guatemala City by 5:30 that afternoon.

By seven o'clock the next morning, we were on our way again, passing over the mountain ranges and the jungle country of Central America. Beautiful trees with splendid bright colors were scattered here and there throughout the vast green forest. What a

274

wonderful sight it was to see. Within an hour, our plane made a stop at San Salvador. Shortly after leaving there, we passed somewhere over the vicinity of El Porventer. I tried to locate it, but was not successful. About nine-thirty a.m. the plane arrived at Tegucigalpa.

After passing through customs, I took a taxi to the Palace Hotel. As soon as possible, I contacted Don Hector Laszio by telephone. That afternoon, I met with him and with Dr. Vargas, another one of the owners of El Porventer. Both of these gentlemen could speak and understand English. They asked about JC. They said they had been concerned about him for some time . . . that JC was determined to get the mill set up and operating before he left. He had just stayed too long.

I learned that the people of Aramecina had cleared a nearby area and built a small landing field. TACI, the local aviation company, operating out of Tegucigalpa, had already tried it out and was ready to do business there. I arranged a flight for the next morning. Jack Scholls, the man JC had left in charge at the mine and Don Domingo were notified by telegraph.

Saturday, February 2nd, after some early morning shopping, Don Hector and I were aboard a TACI plane that took off at 8:45 a.m. It took just one half hour to get to Aramecina. Most everybody from that village and from the nearby countryside were there to greet us. Don Hector, the pilot and I were escorted by the head people to their city headquarters where we were given a royal welcome.

After lunch, Don Hector and the pilot departed for their return trip to Tegucigalpa. Jack Scholls, Don Domingo and I took off for El Porventer on mules. Several hours later we arrived at the mine.

What a change had taken place since my first visit there, back in 1936. Now, there was

OUR MILL, WATER TANK, GAS PLANT & BUNK HOUSE

a nice residence used by Scholls and his family. Then, there was a cook house, a bunk house with a small office located in one end, a shop and the mill. That mill building was quite large. It housed the ore crusher, the mill, amalgamation and concentration tables, a classifier and floatation cells, generators, motors, etc. Adjoining was an assayers room. Then, there was a "Gas Pobre Plant" (wood or other fuel is burned in a furnace to produce gas. The gas is extracted from the fumes, cleaned, then used to power the motors operating the mill and many other machines). The gas power plant was operating, supplying power for the compressor and for agitation of two cyanide tanks.

Jack Donivan and Bill May with a crew were working in the mill, setting up auxilary machinery. I was disappointed not to see Walter Hart. Six months or so back, on different occasions, I had sent two hand-picked men, my friends, who needed work, down to El Porventer. Bill May was a good mechanic and a first class hand about a mine mill. Walter Hart was an engineer and good in a mine. Bill told me Walter didn't get along well with Scholls and had left just about a week before my arrival.

For quarters, I chose to stay in the bunkhouse with Senor Garcia, our bookkeeper, Bill May, and two Manuels, a mine foreman and a mechanic. Jack Donivan shared quarters with Scholls and his family, which included two sons-in-law that worked about the mine.

It was the middle of the dry season and water was exceptionally scarce that year. Scholls had a crew working on a ditch that would bring in more water. There were also crews working in the mine cleaning out old fills and timbering. One group of five men was developing a lime deposit and another was building a kiln. Lime was needed in the operation of the cyanide tanks.

Two of the three cyanide tanks we used to release the gold and silver from the sulphides.

At four o'clock that afternoon, the machinery shut down. It was saturday, payday. Over forty workmen lined up and received their pay . . . one limpera (about fifty cents) per day. That was the standard wage paid daily in Honduras. Shortly thereafter, the camp was quiet. Most of those men took off for their homes in the nearby mountains, or in Aramecina or Caridad. Just four Americans and five or six natives, including the cook remained in camp.

Sunday morning, Scholls and I made an inspection tour of the mine. I needed to get better acquainted with him as much as I needed to check the mine. He was an American, 45 or 50 years old, who had spent the last 15 years or more working in and around mines in Central America. When we were finished with our tour, I felt that I still didn't know much about him. He was a hard man to get friendly with.

That afternoon, Jack Donivan and I checked the mill over. It looked good and Jack felt we would be able to get underway with total operations very soon if there was sufficient water. Later that afternoon, Bill and I took a hike up the ditch to see how it was coming. Considerable work had to be done before we could expect water from that source.

About the middle of the following week, I decided to check the company's books. Senor Garcia was most helpful. I was shocked to find the company owed back wages to many of its former workmen. Some of these debts went back several months. Apparently a habit had been formed of paying only one half of what was owed. Gomez explained that this was done on Scholls' order. He wanted the extra finances to put on more help to push through the work sooner. That way, the mine could get started in full operation quicker. I called Scholls on this and he felt he had done right . . . that all the men would get their money once the mine got rolling (the work crew had averaged 60 men for the past six weeks). With that, I gave Scholls an extra job: pacifying all those creditors when they came in on saturdays to try and collect. That made him mad, but it made Senor Garcia happy. I put an end to that practice immediately.

Work at the mine and the mill was progressing well. Time passed so fast those following weeks. After three weeks had gone by and we hadn't heard a word about our incoming shipment of supplies from the north, so I decided to go to Tegucigalpa to find out why. I also thought I might be able to get some things we needed badly. A message was sent to Aramecina to wire for a plane for ten o'clock the next morning.

Bill and I were on our way early. He had to get certain permits and needed a break. He hadn't been away for over six months. Our plane was on time and our trip to Tegucigalpa was uneventful. We registered at the Palace Hotel, then reported to the Counsel's office. Letters for me had just arrived from Katherine, Al and Lee King. Those letters contained answers for most of my questions.

The news was shocking! Ships on the Pacific Coast runs had been drafted into War-time service and were now hauling supplies to England! All of our supplies were still on the docks at San Pedro and San Francisco! The Grace Line was trying hard to get replacement ships, but so far, without success.

The U.S. Counsel informed Bill and I, that all citizens in foreign countries had been ordered to turn in their passports. Replacements were being issued and would be ready for us in a few days. The War situation didn't look good.

Fortunately, a fair supply of funds had arrived. Now, we could try and pick up some of the supplies we so badly needed. We started on a shopping tour. Bill spoke Spanish so much

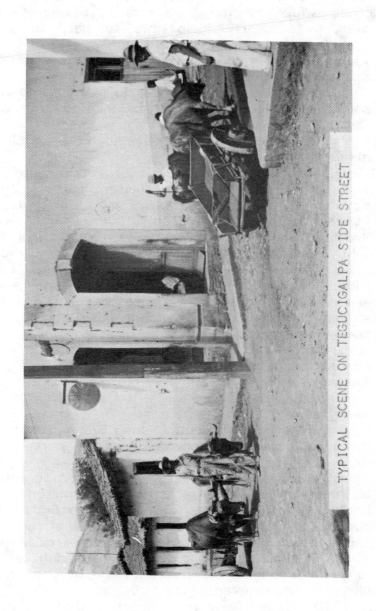

TYPICAL SCENE ON TEGUCIGALPA SIDE STREET

better than I, it sure was good to have him along. Then, we ran into another bit of bad luck. Dynamite, fuse and caps, carbide and other supplies vitally necessary to operate a mine, were nearly impossible to get. It was apparent the shipping problem had caused this shortage. We worked hard at it and did get a small part of what we needed.

We paid Don Hector Laszio a visit and he was glad to see us. For the balance of our stay there, he visited us most every evening. Bill and I got the idea that he enjoyed practicing his English on us.

Then, my old friend Senor Premo paid us a visit. He said he had a pleasant surprise for me and wanted me to go with him the next day. I accompanied him to the office of the Vice President of Honduras and was introduced to that gentleman. After a short but very nice visit, when we were about ready to leave, the Vice President handed me an envelope and asked me to open it. There was an order, signed by the Vice President and bearing the seal of the country, directed to all comandantes or other persons in Honduras, requesting their full cooperation with Paul Nester, in every way possible. I was indeed surprised and thankful. It brought back memories of JC and of the past!

Before we left Tegucigalpa, Bill had all his required papers and, in addition, a permit to carry firearms.

By the time our passports were ready, our business in Tegucigalpa had been completed. We left by truck with over 1000 pounds of supplies. Two of our mozos with a string of pack mules were awaiting us at Hicaro Jilan. The 45 mile trip back through the mountains took three days. We arrived back at the mine late on a friday evening.

JD (Jack Donivan) reported that during our absence, all the auxiliary machinery had been set up and was now operating. The next morning, a saturday, the mill was started up. Three hours later, we ran out of water and had to shut down. A considerable amount of water is used when operating all auxiliary equipment.

That afternoon, as the crew was being paid off, and as Scholls was trying to pacify some of our creditors, he lost his head. He asked me in a very loud voice that most everyone could hear, "Why don't you go back to the States, where you can do some good for the company by keeping funds and supplies coming? You're no good here . . . you can't even speak the language!"

I answered, "Scholls, you're just a plain dam fool, to allow your tongue to run away from your head. You've done a lot of good for the company and we appreciate it, . . . but, we have no use for a man who can't control his tongue. You better pack you're things and get out, you're through!"

Bill May and the two Manuel's were sent to Scholls' place to see that all supplies on hand there was transferred to the store-room in the cookhouse. Scholls would no longer, ever, receive supplies coming through for the mine.

Those three men worked that evening re-enforcing the supply room doors and equipping them with hasps and locks. Senor Garcia would handle the issuance of supplies from that time on.

Scholls pulled out early the next morning . . . Several days later, I was served with a subpoena to answer charges brought by him in the Caridad Court. He wanted his pay and was going to get every bit of it, if he had his way.

The trial date was set some days away. In the evenings, I spent some time preparing. I knew Scholls whould have to take the stand to tell his story. That would make him subject to cross-examination. . . Why not have him tell my story? Who could do it better? . . . I carefully wrote out a cross-examination in English. The answers would tell how El Porventer had recently become developed. Senor Garcia, who was my friend and who had become my interpreter when I needed one, translated that cross-examination into Spanish and I did my practicing on it.

Finally, the day came for court. How the word got around, I don't know, but most all the head people from Aramecina, plus those who could get away from the mine, were there. I think most everyone from Caridad was there too. That court room couldn't hold them all.

Court was called. Everybody was surprised when I insisted on handling my own defense. Senor Garcia was at my side. Scholls did his thing as I had expected. Then I cross-examined. Scholls' answers told the story of how El Porventer came to be developed. I believe I did a good job. He was shocked! The court, of course, found in his favor, but put off payment for three months. Then, the hearing would be to see what the situation at El Porventer might be at that time. It didn't take long for Sholls to disappear from Caridad after that trial.

Our small group from the mine was invited to attend a celebration. What a party that turned out to be! Old time square dancing and the guaro (distilled sugar-cane) flowing freely. It was the next afternoon before we were ready to return to the mine. An escort of many horsemen accompanied us on our way for the first several miles. After they left us, I had the feeling that now, we had many friends in Caridad.

At El Porventer, the shortage of water held us back. We could only operate the mill three or four hours each day. The crew was still working on the ditch, but it looked like we would have to wait for the rain season to get more water. When operating, the mill made

GAS POWER PLANT & BUNK HOUSE

concentrates. Whenever an oxcart or mule freighter was headed towards the coast, we would send our concentrates for trans-shipment to the smelter at Selby, Washington.

I started worrying. What if the Grace Line was unable to replace those coastal ships? Without ships, we would never be able to get our concentrates to the smelter. What would we do?

The only answer that I could come up with was to get an assay furnace and do our own assaying. That way, we could at least make our own recovery of the free gold. JD (Jack Donivan) said he could build the assay furnace if he had the materials. We already had the gas plant and air compressor. He made up a drawing and a list of the materials needed.

Then our gas plant broke down and I had to go to Tegucigalpa for parts. JD was placed in charge and early the next morning, I was on my way with one of our mozos. We brought with us a pack mule loaded with ore samples to be assayed.

The trip, though a tough one, was always interesting. We traveled the first forty-five miles mule-back, through the mountains. I marveled at the orchids growing on the lower branches of the pines. Exquisite birds entertained us with their unusual songs. At times, monkeys in the tops of trees, accompanied us, traveling along as porpoises do with ships at sea. On occasion, we saw boa-constrictors. I was told, that's why the natives carried their macheties in their hands at all times and not in a scabbard.

When we reached the higher altitudes, underbrush became as thick as it is in Western Oregon. Wild blackberries were abundant. If you strayed off the trail, you wouldn't travel far.

The trail ended at a small village on the main road from San Lorenzo on the Pacific Coast to Tegucigalpa. Our mozo left with the mules to return to the mine. Later, I would send for him when I was ready to return. . . I made arrangements with a truck driver for transportation to the capital. This was necessary as busses were so few . Each truck driver would make his own deal and the exchange of produce or most anything was usually accepted in lieu of money. I have never known a prospective passenger being turned down.

Once, I was on a truck headed towards Tegucigalpa. The truck was loaded with supplies and had ten passengers up on top. We came onto the sight of an accident. Another truck, traveling in the opposite direction blew a tire and went over the bank, down about fifty feet. That truck had been carrying about twenty passengers. Luckily, no one was injured! Everybody from both trucks went to work. As the natives worked, they sang, told funny stories and really enjoyed themselves. It was quite a sight. After four or five hours, the truck was back on the road and ready to go. There was with everyone a feeling of happy pride. At no time was any payment either offered or asked for. When they parted, each said "adios" like the parting of old time friends.

Upon arrival at Tegucigalpa, I took care of my business at the repair shops and at the assayers and then picked up my mail. There were letters from Katherine and from Al. I also received some funds from Al and felt pretty good about that. Anything I received from now on would indeed be a pleasant surprise.

Hoping to get some help in the way of advise, I contacted the manager of El Rodolpho mine. He invited me out. When I told him I needed a head foreman, he suggested I contact the Anna Maria mine. Then he took me to their assay office. They were using a furnace like we had in mind. When I left there, I had a drawing of it.

The manager of the Anna Maria mine put me in touch with Francisco Taylor, a Honduran who had immigrated from Switzerland. He was a friendly man and I was favorably impressed with him. When told of all the problems at El Porventer, he was willing to take a chance with us.

Taylor helped me in locating supplies we needed badly. He even helped me find a proper place to eat while I was in Tegucigalpa. He took me to an orphanage that operated a dining room for some of the business men of Tegucigalpa. A German lady cook supplied these gentlemen with the most wonderful food at reasonable prices. Fourteen or fifteen year old orphan girls served as waitresses. After eating there, I knew where I would go for my meals from that time on.

One day, I met an American, Robert Higgins, a civil engineer who had charge of road construction for the Honduran government. He invited me to his quarters to look at some ore samples. You should have seen the supply of rocks he had in that large corner hotel room. That bachelor's hobby was rock collecting. Cutting roads through the mountains uncovered interesting veins. Some day, he might make a rich discovery.

Jack Donivan, who was supposed to be in charge back at the mine, showed up at my hotel. He had placed Bill May in charge and he had his wife with him. I didn't even know that he was married. His wife was a Costa Rican and had come to El Porventer to take her husband home. She explained, they could go on no longer under the circumstances and with the conditions existing at the mine as well as world-wide. I believe I understood about how she felt. JD said he expected no pay at the time. He knew just what our financial situation was. We wished each other well and they departed. I have never seen either one of them since.

At the assayer's, I went over the results of our last sample lot. Between us, we worked out a system, by code, where I could get reports on his assays without coming to Tegucigalpa. I would keep samples coming to him and via telegraph-code he would send me the results. Also, if necessary, he could send me an important message by code.

Then, I received another letter from Al. He said, that due to the War, a Presidential Order had been issued, directed to all operators of mines! "Necessary supplies are to be sold only to operators of mines producing strategic metals! Those not producing strategic metals are to be closed down and their employees urged to get work in mines producing essential metals in short supply!" I hated to think about just how that would affect our financing. Al also said he had located an assayer willing to come, but it would be ten days or more before he could leave.

When Taylor and I headed out early the next morning, I was feeling pretty low. We did have a fair sized load of freight with us. Upon arrival at the mine, I called a meeting of all those considered important. Don Domingo, Senor Garcia, Bill May, Francisco Taylor and the two Manuels. I gave them the news and we discussed the situation. It was concluded, our only chance would be to find "High Grade." If we could get by until the assayer arrived, our chances would improve 100%. Meanwhile, I would keep samples traveling towards Tegucigalpa . . . but that was slow and expensive.

Our main crew was laid off. Don Domingo would work with his small group in the mine. Taylor would familiarize himself in the mine and help otherwise as he could. One of the Manuels, the mine foreman, pulled out. The other Manuel stayed to help as he could. Senor Garcia explained, he wanted to remain with us, but his wife in Tegucigalpa was about to have a baby and he wanted to be with her.

Time went by fast for the first few days. Then, things started happening. Our cook took off one night and everything loose around the cookhouse went with her. I found myself spending more time trying to pacify creditors than in doing useful work. During this period, I was served with three more subpoenas. One from Caridad and two from Aramecina. In each case, I made the necessary appearances and, fortunately, was able to get thirty day extensions.

Then word finally came. Our assayer would be arriving in Tegucigalpa. Bill May was left in charge and I went to meet him. I don't know why, but for some reason, I decided to travel the low-land route. The rain season was just starting so I didn't expect hazardous river crossings. Crossing the Aramecina River, I was nearly carried away! Then, when I got to the Nacaome, I crossed that river in what they called a canoe. It was a light circular frame, covered with skins and could be compared to a large round wash tub. You took a paddle stroke on one side and then on the other to make any headway.

After arriving in Tegucigalpa and cleaning up, I picked up my mail. There was a letter from Katherine and one from Al. Bad news from Katherine . . . her father had passed away. Besides that, she had been forced to sell our home. She and the girls would be going to Portland to live with her sister, Margaret Arata. From Al, I got a little boost. He had forwarded some funds and said a Mr. Boyle, an assayer, would be in on the plane next morning.

It was near noon and I was very hungry. I made my way to the special eating place. When I entered the dining room, it was about half full. As I took my seat, for some reason, I got the feeling that I wasn't wanted. I was hungry and had been looking forward to this meal for some time. Rapidly, the dining room filled and as each additional person came into that room, I got critical glances. These glances, followed by very soft German conversation, gave me the feeling they were talking about me. . . but I was hungry. I ordered anyway.

My meal was brought in and it was all I had hoped for. I went to work on it and stopped being concerned about the coldness of my fellow diners, for the moment.

Suddenly, a new arrival, a stranger to me entered the dining room. Every man in that room, except me, jumped to his feet, threw up his right arm and greeted the newcomer with a "Heil Hitler!" He "Heil Hitlered" right back! Then he glared at me like a mad man and blasted off in German! I guess its just as well I didn't understand a word. I kept right on eating, perhaps a bit faster. I wasn't going to let that bunch beat me out of a meal that I had been looking forward to for so long.

Late that afternoon, upon returning to my hotel, there was a message for me from Walter Gage, United States Counsel at Tegucigalpa.

"Paul, would like to see you as soon as possible. W.G."

I went to the Counsel's office immediately.

"Hi, Paul. I hear you finally found a good place to eat."

"Yes, I did . . . but after my experience at noon today, I don't know whether its worthwhile or not."

"Well, if I were you, I'd go back to the fried beans and tortillas. You're going to miss the good food, but over the long run, I think it would be a lot healthier for you. Why did you have to arrive back in town, just when Adolph's messenger boy brings important news from the Fatherland?"

Senor Hector Laszio paid me a visit. From the start, he had been one of our strongest backers. Besides being a part owner of El Porventer, don Hector's family owned and operated the import-export firm at Amapala. All shipments to and from the mine, went through his company. Naturally, he wanted very much to see us succeed. Now, there were no ships . . . soon it looked like there would be no mine. We spent considerable time swapping the blues.

Later, I went over to pay a visit to my friend, Robert Higgert. He was not there. Inquiring at the hotel office, I was told Mr. Higgert was sick in the hospital. Even the doctors couldn't figure out what was wrong with him. It was something most unusual.

Late that evening, I was served with two separate subpoenas for appearances in the court at Tegucigalpa. I needed help. Contacting Senor Premo, I asked if he could recommend a good attorney. Early the next morning, Senor Premo took me to the offices of attorney Durman and I told that gentleman what my troubles were. Durman was a man who came right to the point. He got out a Spanish Penal Code. Opening it to a certain page, he said, read. There, in very plain words it stated that a debtor could be thrown in prison and held until the debt was paid. This was the Old Spanish Law. I asked for an opinion as to whether this applied to me as manager of a corporation. His answer was, "I have no doubt, it would apply." Senor Durman then agreed to represent me in court and if possible get a 30 day extension in each case.

Later that morning, I picked up Mr. Boyle, the assayer. He had a rough trip and would appreciate a rest overnight.

This gave me a chance to do some writing. For some time a plan had been forming in my mind. Now, it was time to start putting it into operation. I needed money to get out of that country and I needed it fast. Also, there was reason to believe my mail was being censored.

I wrote a letter to Katherine with a duplicate for Al, detailing instructions of what I wanted. No mistakes could be made on this next move, so I took my letters to the U.S. Counsel's office and the originals were mailed in Counselor's envelopes. The duplicates were taken to a good friend and mailed in envelopes of that man's firm.

Early the next morning Boyle and I were on our way with supplies. This time with a light load. I did have a carefully packed set of gold scales which the assayer would need. We traveled a new route, through the mountains, through Curarean Indian territory. This was my first time this way and it took one day longer. The traveling was rough, but it was through beautiful country. I was well pleased with the way my friend was taking this trip. It was pretty rugged for a city man.

Upon arrival at the mine, I got another shock. Bill May had left. There was a note saying that he was sorry, but, he didn't see how we had a chance and he was leaving while the going was good. I knew he was broke and it's a long long way to the good old U.S.A. I made a silent prayer that he would make it.

While I was gone, our small mill had been set up. Now it was ready for operation, when, and if Don Domingo had been able to produce some amalgum. The gold had been sent to San Salvador and traded for carbide and quick-silver.

Boyle and I checked over the assay furnace. Then, we made a trip through the mine and again through the mill. Our assayer wasn't much of a talker, but I had the feeling he was impressed.

Next morning, we (Boyle, Manuel and I) tried to get the Pobre Plant going. We needed the gas for the compressor and the assay furnace. The wet wood gave us troubles, but before that day was finished, we had learned how to cope with it. By the end of the second day, Boyle was getting the hang of things pretty well. For the next week, we worked hard, trying not just for the commercial run of ore, but for "High Grade."

COUNTY OF LOS ANGELES

SHERIFF

LOS ANGELES, CALIFORNIA

July 21, 1928.

Deputy Paul Nester
Temple Sub Station # 5
Temple, Calif.

Sir:

Pursuant to orders of July 21st., 1928, issued by WILLIAM I. TRA[ ] Sheriff, per R. H. Wright, Chief Criminal Deputy, you are relieved fr[ ] duty at Temple Sub Station # 5, effective 8:00 A.M. Sunday, July 22n[ ] as you will be through with your shift at that time.

You are assigned to duty at Sherman Sub Station # 9, to serve und[ ] Capt. Hanby.

Personally, I regret very much to lose you as a member of this Station and wish you the best of success in your new duties. If I car[ ] be of service to you at any time, please call on me. I had no previou[ ] knowledge of these orders.

R. M. Conly, Captain
Temple Station # 5

RMC/WHJ

CHAPTER 20

ESCAPE

1941

One day, it was necessary for me to face up to six Curarean Indians. They were loggers who had supplied timbers for the construction of our mill. They had not been paid and had vowed they were going to collect. Each one had a machete in his hand! While swinging those machetes, they told me what was going to happen to me if they didn't get their money! I told them that they might get me, but, my .44 had six slugs in it and I would promise that at least three or four of them would never swing a machete again! Guess they knew I meant it, for they backed off and said they would return.

That evening, Boyle pulled out. He hired one of the natives to guide him across the border to San Salvador.

The next day, our Gas Pobre plant was embargoed (seized by law).

Two days later I received two telegrams . . . the telegrams I had been waiting for. I was glad I had set up the code . . . now it was time to move.

The balance of that day was spent

preparing for my last departure from El Porventer. I thought it was necessary to leave the impression that I was just making my usual trip to Tegucigalpa for funds and supplies. Our mozo was ordered to bring up a certain mule (a good traveler in the dark) with some feed, so that the mule would be well fed and ready for a very early departure in the morning.

Instead, shortly after dark, that mule and I were on our way. I knew the moon would be up about ten o'clock and I could travel all night. Another thing, I didn't want anyone to see which route I was taking or know what load I was carrying. I kept away from Aramecina and Caridad. Traveling nights only, I made my way to Hicaro Joran and left the mule at the usual place. I didn't wait long before a passing truck stopped for me. I arrived in Tegucigalpa late the afternoon of the third day.

Cleaning up, I had supper then went to the Counsel's office. It was closed and the doors were locked. My assayer friend was not to be found either. So I wandered over to Mr. Higgert's hotel and found him at home. He was well on his way to recovery after being in the hospital. He explained to me, his trouble had been general aches and pains all over and the loss of good use of his arms and legs. Even after two weeks at the hospital, the doctors couldn't find out just what the cause was. At the hospital, however, he steadily improved and finally was able to return to his hotel room. There, he found the maid had taken advantage of his absence. She had cleaned out all the boxes of rocks from under his bed and had stacked them neatly under the dog's bed. Within a few days, the little bulldog that Higgert loved so much got sick. He couldn't hardly stand. He must have looked about like how Higgert felt when they took him to the hospital! Could it be because of those rocks under the bed?

Right away, Higgert had a small box made up that was light proof. He then purchased some photo films and, in the dark, placed one film in the bottom of the box, over a sheet of white paper. Using string, a key was hung horizontally above the film. Then a good sized piece of rock from under the dog's bed was attached inside the top of the box. The box was closed tightly and placed in a dark closet. Two days later, the box was opened. The film was taken out and examined. You should have seen the picture on the white paper. The rock was RADIO-ACTIVE! All the rock in that room was put out. Within a few days, Higgert and his dog, both, were well on their way to recovery.

Up early after a good night's sleep, I stopped at my assayer friend and left the gold scale that had been carefully packed and brought from the mine. Then I proceeded on to the Counsel's office.

Walter Gage greeted me, "Paul, it's so good to see you again. How are you?"

"I'm all right. How are you and what's this urgent business you mentioned in your telegram?"

"You know, Paul, these machete affairs are so messy! I'm happy to see you in such good health!"

Then, it came to me . . . he knew about that affair at the mine. But how did he find out? So I asked him.

His answer was, "Well, it's our business to know what's going on. Especially with our own people." He hesitated, then he said, "Why don't you level with me Paul? What's your plan?"

I only paused momentarily. Then, I told him, "In a day or so, I'll head back to El Porventer as I usually do. Only this time, I'll get lost in the mountains on my way back. I'll make my way to the capital at El Salvador. There, funds are awaiting me at the U.S.

Counsel's office. With those funds, I'll be able to make my way back to the States."

Gage hesitated, then asked, "What if you get away for a while. Then, they pick you up somewhere between San Salvador and the United States border? There won't be much chance of us helping you then. I have a plan too. Why don't you listen to my plan."

I agreed to listen.

Gage went to the phone and called Senor Garcia, our former bookkeeper and my friend. He told Senor Garcia that I was in his office and that I needed help, would he come over. When Garcia arrived Gage told him, "Paul has to go to the States to obtain funds for the completion of work at El Porventer. He has worked hard to develop that mine and its success depends upon arranging more and better financing. In order to leave this country, Paul has to get his passport stamped by four different government departments. We have reason to believe, he may have difficulty! Would you go with him? If he has trouble, tell the officer in that department why Paul is leaving. Also tell him, the U.S. Counsel is interested in seeing that Paul gets to go. If it is necessary, the American Counsel will pay a visit to the President of Honduras, to see that he gets legal clearance to leave this country."

Senor Garcia was willing to help and soon we were on our way.

We had no difficulty in three of the departments, but in the last one, a HOLD had been placed for me! We were in the Office of Internal Affairs for nearly an hour. Finally, the head of that department gave in and my passport was stamped.

Thank God for Garcia. He did his bit and he did it well. Returning to Walter Gage's office, we reported our success. Gage looked at his watch. It was just noon. He said, "There's a Pan American airliner coming through on its

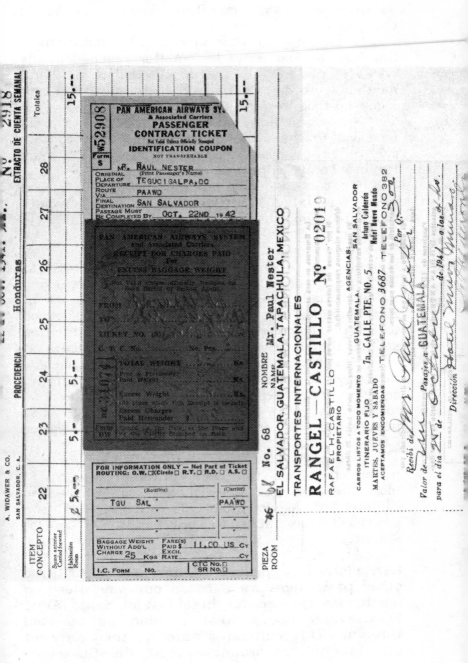

way north. It's due to leave here for San Salvador at 2:15 p.m. Paul, you better be on that plane."

I told him, I was sorry, but I didn't have the fare to San Salvador. Walter reached in his pocket, pulled out a twenty dollar bill and handed it to me. I thanked him and Garcia and I lost no time in departing.

After picking up my belongings, Garcia took me to the airport. He promised to contact my other friends and tell them why I was leaving Tegucigalpa in such a hurry.

That wednesday, October 22, 1941, the plane was late. The trip to San Salvador only took fifty minutes. This time, I was able to make out Caridad, as we passed over the Curarean area. At San Salvador I was transported to the Nueva Mundo Hotel. It was too late to go to the Counsel's office, so I walked, had supper, then walked some more. San Salvador was an up-to-date city compared to Tegucigalpa. The part of a residential section that I was able to see, was very nice.

The next morning, after breakfast, I made my way to the Counsel's office. Identifying myself, I picked up the $100 Katherine had forwarded. A money order for $20 was purchased and sent back to my friend Walter Gage.

After that, I had pictures taken for the permit required to travel through Mexico. I took the bus out to Little Mexico, where the Minister of Mexico had his offices. For two pesos, I was able to purchase my Tourist Permit.

At 4:30 a.m. the next morning, the Carmalleta Bus picked me up and with three other passengers we were on our way. Heading north, we stopped for breakfast at Santa Ann. For several hours, that morning we traveled through richly cultivated country, then we went up through the mountains. At the Guatemala border, the usual checking was in order. There was no trouble, just the delay. Late that afternoon, we arrived at Guatemala City and I registered at the Grand Hotel. After supper that evening, I did my usual walking and sight-seeing. Guatemala is a very interesting place to visit and I enjoyed it there.

The next morning, a railroad ticket was purchased to the Mexican border south of Tapachula. It cost $2.65 for a second class fare. Those railroad tracks were narrow gage and the equipment was old. It had been discarded by United States railroads about 1910. The oak seats were mighty hard and as the miles slowly went by, they got harder.

We finally arrived at the end of the tracks, the border between Guatemala and Mexico. All passengers going on north, had to walk one mile to the customs and immigration station. After passing that hurdle, we crossed the river in a poling boat. Arriving in Sachote, Mexico, we passed through Mexican customs. That night, I stayed at the Sachote hotel. It turned out to be the lousiest place I have ever spent a night.

Next morning at 6:30 a.m., I was aboard a train headed for Vera Cruz. Another second class ticket was purchased. This train was better, but still had those hard wooden seats. Also, this train traveled so very slowly . . . I believe it was worse than that "Slow train through Arkansas." They said it was due to the wet season. Perhaps it was . . . because, as we approached every bridge or trestle, the engine would stop, then slowly start up and make the crossing. They did get up a speed of about six miles an hour, just right for jogging and that's just what several of us did, to get some exercise. At Tapachula, we picked up quite a few passengers. Now, every seat was taken and baggage was stacked in the passageways. It was a good idea to make friends with your neighbors, because, if you had moved from your seat, you might not have been able to get back in when you returned.

I believe that train must have stopped about every twenty minutes. Indian natives, with oodles of baggage would get on or off. If you had any baggage, it kept you busy trying to keep track of it. Daytime was tough, but when it came to the night, it really got bad.

Most of this low-land country was in the banana belt. Rich plantations, probably owned by one of the large fruit companies. The natives, all, seemed to be working and happy. They tried hard to be congenial and good traveling companions. I liked them.

After several days of this kind of travel, we arrived at Vera Cruz. The Terminal Hotel was located in the railroad station. I took a room, had a good shower and went to bed. I slept soundly until nine o'clock the next morning. The next train north didn't leave until that evening, so I was able to see quite a bit of the town.

Vera Cruz had been a busy and prosperous city. Now, only two ships were in port and the people were not very happy about this. Business was slow and there were not many people on the streets.

That afternoon, I purchased another second class ticket to Mexico City. The train left at seven o'clock. That night was better than the others. We still had those hard seats, but there were not so many passengers and that train traveled faster. We arrived in Mexico City about seven o'clock the next morning. The next train out for the north was at 11:50 a.m. Again, I purchased a second class ticket and again, I got those same hard seats.

Now, we were traveling through plateau country between high mountain ranges. Occasionally the train would stop at some small village or town for thirty minutes or so. Indian vendors, with baskets of food on their heads were peddling their wares to hungry passengers. The meal time was a fun time and everybody enjoyed it. Everything I bought tasted good. However, north of Mexico City, I noticed there wasn't as much fruit as there had been in the south.

Early the morning of November 1, 1941, our train arrived at the bridge between Jurez, Mexico and El Paso, Texas. Immigration and Customs Officers came aboard and checked our passports and baggage. By nine o'clock that was completed and the train crossed over from Mexico to the United States. What a wonderful feeling.

When I got off the train, I felt like falling to the ground and kissing the soil . . . It was so good to be back in my own country, and in good health.

Making a careful search of my pockets, I came up with a total of seventy three cents. I had my .44 Smith and Wesson and it didn't take me long to find a hawk shop. Minutes later, I came out with $20 and the fare to Los Angeles was only $11. That evening I boarded a bus for Los Angeles, traveled all night and arrived the next morning. A street car took me on out to Monica and Al's. Back home in the good old United States. THANK GOD I MADE IT!

P.S. Perhaps three months after my arrival back in Los Angeles, I received a letter from Bill May which had been mailed in Guatemala. In his letter, Bill told me that some months before, as he was hitch-hiking north on one of the roads through Guatemala, a car stopped and the driver offered him a ride. Tired, hungry and broke, he was glad to accept. The driver, a middle-aged man was friendly and took Bill to his hacienda. After eating a good meal, Bill discovered a violin on the fireplace mantle. He asked permission to examine it. Bill started to play. He had never even told me that he had left home because his mother was trying to make a concert violinist of him.

Anyway, the music attracted the beautiful daughter of his new-found friend. He went on to tell me how nice the daughter was and how big that rancho was. He said he would be staying there for a while.

I'll bet he's still there and loving every bit of it. Good for you Bill, you deserve it.

The official publishing date is December 10, 1983.
However, the First Half of My Life is available now.
Write to:

        Willamette Press
        P.O. Box 2065
        Beaverton, Oregon
              97075

Please include check or money order for prompt
delivery: Hardback $14.95 each
           Paperback $9.95 each.
Add sales tax if it is required in your state.